MY LIFE IN FOOTBALL

My Life in Football
Hunter Davies

MAINSTREAM
PUBLISHING

First published in Great Britain 1990 by
MAINSTREAM PUBLISHING COMPANY (EDINBURGH) LTD
7 Albany Street
Edinburgh EH1 3UG

British Library Cataloguing in Publication Data

Davies, Hunter *1936–*
    My life in football.
    1. Great Britain. Association football
    I. Title
    796.334

    ISBN 1-85158-320-5

Typeset in Garamond by Novatext Graphix, Edinburgh
Printed in Great Britain by Billings and Sons, Worcester

For my brother Johnny,
still playing, lucky beggar

Acknowledgments

I am grateful to the editors of *The Sunday Times, The Times, Punch, The Independent*, and *The Mail on Sunday's YOU* magazine for reproduction permissions. Most of these pieces first appeared in their publications. One or two are unpublished, such as the Kevin Keegan profile. (I went to Hamburg to see him and returned to find *The Sunday Times* closed for a year, so it never made it.) Mostly they are original, longer versions of what appeared at the time. Over these last 25 years of writing about football, I am particularly indebted to Harry Evans, former editor of *The Sunday Times* and *The Times*, for his encouragement when I was on *The Glory Game* trail; to Charlie Burgess of *The Independent* for his encouragement, of me and Carlisle United; and to Nick Gordon of *YOU* magazine, for sending me to Cameroon. And to Jake, for coming to matches and giving me the benefit of his enormous knowledge of Italian football.

Contents

Introduction

THE TITLE is a bit of cheek. I admit it. How can I pretend I've had a life in football when I've never been a professional player? Real footballers, and real managers,can become very upset when outsiders dare to comment and carp and criticise. They like to think that only those who have done it are equipped to understand. Once you have performed, then you can pontificate. But many lives revolve in and around football, without the need to get out onto the park and do it for a living.I like to think I have experienced quite a few of them.

Firstly, as a punter. I started, as we mostly do , on the terraces as a boy.When I made it as an adult, I dragged along my own son (and daughter – this is the modern age). It began with Carlisle United, my home town, then Spurs took over in the 1960s when I had moved to London. There's a lot about both teams in this book,but then it is my book.You will have your clubs you have followed,but the passions – and the despairs – of the ordinary punters are very much the same.

I also played. Not the real stuff of course, just little local leagues when I was young. At the age of around 30, something more unusual happened. I began my own team, as you will discover. That was a Football Life all on its own which at one time dominated my whole week till the inevitable happened. Then for many years I was a football journalist, reporting matches, interviewing our heroes, looking out for new trends, new happenings in the wonderful world of football. I've also been a columnist, in *Punch* and then the *Independent,* using any excuse to drag in my love for football.

I edged a bit deeper into things by becoming a football author, producing a whole book on football called *The Glory Game,* following a year in the life of a First Division team. Okay, it was Spurs, but I like to think it could have been any top club. It is now something of a classic, at least it gets reprinted all the time.There are no excerpts from it in this book (Go on, rush out and buy the original) but I have included a long piece I wrote for the *Sunday Times* about a day with the team on the way to a match, which was a trial run for the book to see if I could get access to the players and the dressing-room.

The strange thing about these several lives I have led in football is that over the last 25 years they have each changed and developed in their own way. In arranging the various types of articles chronologically, as they roughly appeared, I discovered looking back at them that a sort of narrative has emerged, which I was not aware of at the time.

The book begins in 1965 with one of our all time superstars, G. Best. How young and innocent he sounded that day I met him. Not even drinking. Then we observe other stars appearing, some to disappear very quickly. Through them you can see the world of football gradually changing . The money, for a start. They were on £50 a week just 25 years ago, and often took summer jobs to eke out their pay. Eventually, the millionaire footballers arrive, and our very first, Kevin Keegan, is included in the book. Graeme Souness is probably even richer, with his own shares in Rangers. He makes two appearances. I've met him thrice in my football life – at Spurs as a boy in the Seventies, in Italy as a star with Sampdoria in the Eighties, and in 1990 as a manager running Rangers. Where will he be in ten years time?

The commercialisation of football is a running theme, trickling quietly at first, then it turns into a flood with the arrival of the first agents, the sponsors, the executive boxes, the satellite TV rights, till it now seems that football is more about making money than pleasing punters.

Mainly, though, it's about the players, their stories and struggles, their worries and wonders, the homegrown as well as the imported variety. One of the earliest black players was Clyde Best, long before black players took such a leading role in our national game. I was also there to see Ossie Ardiles in his first game. He was among the earliest of our foreign players.

There are several managers included, two who have run England, plus Brian Clough. Note well how Clough said that at the age of 55 – which he is now – he could not possibly see himself still in football.

I had forgotten I ever interviewed Steve Heighway, one of our first graduate players. His honesty is still remarkable. What he told me that day would have him fined by most clubs today. And he's not very complimentary either about Bill Shankly, then his manager, now turned into a legend.

You will notice, as the years go on, a certain personal change in me. Not just the old bones, but the old passions creaking. I could never have imagined, back in 1965, that I would ever say I HATE SPURS. It's part of any love affair to have fits of hate. I'm amazed it took so long.

But this book is basically about LOVE – a love affair with football over these last 25 years, the pleasures and the pains, the sort many of us have experienced as we watch the passing show of our national game.

PS – As the world now knows, Cameroon were the sensation of the 1990 World Cup. In their first match they beat Argentina (including Maradona), then went on to beat Rumania and Columbia. They were eliminated in the quarter-finals, rather luckily, by England. Hurry, hurry to page 171.

Hunter Davies
July 1990

1965

Georgy Boy

GEORGE BEST is a very shy, quiet boy, of nineteen. He has a soft Belfast accent and a Beatle haircut. His wage for the week before last was £175.

Mr Best plays for Manchester United and is the boy wonder of football.

'When I first went to the ground and I'd seen all those big lads, I thought, there's no chance here. I'll never make the grade. I was fifteen and sharing digs with another Belfast boy. After two weeks, I packed up and went home. I was just so homesick.

'But my father talked me into coming back, and I stayed. I've changed a lot since those days. If somebody in a shop gave me change out of ten bob and I'd given them a pound, I'd be too shy to complain.

'You've got to have confidence to be a footballer. I think in the last two months I've got it. I used to lie in my bed on Friday nights, imagining how I was going to beat everybody. Funny, I never did badly, always well, when I was doing this thinking. Now I never think about the match at all.

'I used to wear very quiet clothes. Now, if I see something smart, no matter what anybody else says, I buy it. I've got a black and white striped jacket. The lads in the team are always saying, " Here comes the butcher."

'I used to write home three or four times a week. Now, well, I haven't written at all for a few weeks, it's terrible. That's one thing I've gone down on.

'But I can talk to my parents, the way I never used to, as if I'm grown up. I can talk about girls. I never had the nerve before.

'I thought I wouldn't be able to talk to Denis Law and Bobby Charlton, the ones I'd always hero-worshipped as a kid. But your opinion changes. They're just like ordinary blokes in the street.

'They're all married in the first team, so after training I get a bit bored. I thought at first they didn't want me to mix. They do, but they've got families. The afternoons, I either play snooker or go bowling. Pictures perhaps twice a week. I'm getting very lazy. I read a bit. Horror stories, comics, that sort of thing.

'I don't drink or smoke. Perhaps on a rare occasion, I might have a lager. Then it gets back to the boss, Mr Busby, that you're drunk. I share digs with another footballer. I would like to have a flat on my own. But the boss thinks there might be temptation. Perhaps, when I'm twenty-one. I've no complaints. I like my landlady.

13

'One thing you never realise until you actually play, is that other footballers are always talking to you on the pitch, though no one else can hear. One bloke every time he got near me said, get your hair cut, scruff. They try to nark you, break you down.

'I've found that footballers never read reports of their own matches. They're just not interested. They *know* what happened. I read them. I'm young.

'I save most of my money. Last week's £175 was very unusual—I had three matches, one an international. Often it's down to £50 a week.

'What I'd like to be is a millionaire, that's what I'd like. If it meant not playing football again from this minute on? Well, perhaps I don't want to be a millionaire after all.'

1966

World Cup Willies

THIS IS World Cup year. Football teams from 16 nations will come to England in July to play against each other for a 12-inch-high solid gold cup weighing nine pounds.

The sale of tickets for the matches will come to more than one and a half million pounds. The Football Association's share of the profits will be 25 per cent.

But the biggest money of all will be made by the commercial boys who are cashing in like mad on the World Cup. As a merchandising gimmick, it is even bigger than James Bond or Noddy.

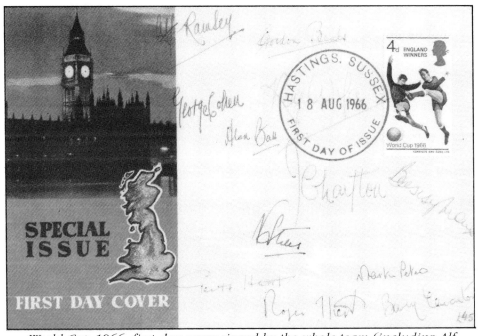

World Cup 1966: first-day cover signed by the whole team (including Alf Ramsey – not normally known for his joined up writing)

In the next few months, over £4 million worth of goods will be flooding the market all stamped with some sort of World Cup insignia. The FA will get about £200,000 of this in royalties.

I woz there: my ticket for the World Cup final 1966

World Cup Willie, the cartoon figure with the Union Jack on his back, will be everywhere. He was the idea of Walter Tuckwell's, the firm which is handling the licensing rights on behalf of the FA. (The FA's idea is the World Cup Insignia – a rather dull picture of the World Cup with the Union Jack in the background.)

If you have an idea for a World Cup product, you go along to Tuckwell's for permission, pay a down payment and agree to pay a royalty of around five per cent of the manufacturing cost. So far, say Tuckwell's, about the only products missing are jock straps and cigarettes.

They're in two minds about cigarettes – it could mean a lot of money, but they are a bit worried about the smoking scare.

Everything else seems to have been thought of, from Lonnie Donegan's

World Cup Willie song to the World Cup Beer which Watneys are doing.

There are also World Cup Willie braces ties, track suits, T-shirts, baseball caps (for football?), autograph books, toffees, potato crisps, table cloths, football games, knitting patterns and periscopes. Not to mention the World Cup Willie Soft Plush Doll, World Cup Willie Self-Adhesive Suspending Clips, World Cup Willie TV Snowstorms and World Cup Willie Rollykins, whatever they are.

There is a showroom in Holborn in which all these delights will be on show and of course there will be lots of other shops in the World Cup Village at Wembley.

There is even a dwarf who dresses up as a live World Cup Willie and is available for all sales promotions from five guineas an hour. There have been a few pirates. Somebody had the nerve to put World Cup tea-towels on the market without permission – but Tuckwell's soon stopped that. One of the smartest ideas, which should make a great deal of money, is the World Cup Willie Collectors' Club. It's surprising that the FA didn't organise this one themselves. You pay five bob to join the club and get in return a badge, monthly bulletins about the World Cup and the chance of all sorts of World Cup paraphernalia at reduced prices.

Graham Bateson, an ex-adman who plays for Corinthian Casuals, and two others run the club from cramped offices above a Wimpy Bar in Kensington High Street. So far they have about 5,000 members. They expect to have 100,000 by July.

He started a special recruiting drive in France and got 1,000 new members in a week. He finds the average age of the French fans is 20, whereas the English average is about 12. Which proves something.

1967

Glasgow Glows

THIS WEEK, Glasgow Celtic become the first British team to play in the final of the European Cup. Next week, Glasgow Rangers play in the final of the European Cup Winners' Cup. This domination by Glasgow of European football leaves England, with its little local conflicts like the FA Cup final, rather out in the cold.

When Celtic and Rangers win their Saturday games, most Glasgow factories report that production on Monday morning is 15 per cent higher than if they lose. This season Glasgow production managers have all had contented scowls.

On Saturdays, late afternoon sales of the sports editions of the local *Evening Citizen* and *Evening Times* go up by several thousands if the teams win. This year, both are enjoying booming circulations.

Just as the World Cup victory gave England such pleasure, a new pride and a new confidence, which was reflected at many levels of English life, so the hot flush of success is now spreading through the whole of Scotland. For Rangers and Celtic are national teams. Every Protestant boy in Scotland wants to play for Rangers. Every good little Catholic wants to play for Celtic.

Up to now, the English have always been more aware of the freakish aspects of Glasgow football rather than the sport – how many Rangers and Celtic supporters got killed or arrested on New Year's Day? (The record number of arrests, incidentally, still stands at 128, during the 1925 match, which rather dis proves that the violence has been getting worse.)

Soccer in Scotland always has been a social phenomenon, though up to now it has seemed curiously dated. The Rangers Celtic cult has been reminiscent of the pre-war adulation of Arsenal. Since the war, in the affluent South, there have been other things for people to think about. An ambitious Southern kid these days knows there are many ways of making £100 a week and getting on. He can be a photographer, hair stylist or pop singer. So who wants to be a footballer?

The long-established Scottish tradition of football as a way up in life has had few rivals, which is why Scotland still produces more top players proportionally than England. Even in yesterday's *English* Cup final, six out of the 22 players were Scottish. (The ratio of Scots to English nationally is 1:11.)

But footballers no longer have to leave Scotland to get opportunities and big money. Celtic, who have always been rather poor financially, now have 16 players earning over £5,000 a year. No English team can do better than that.

If Celtic win on Thursday, they will be able to call themselves the best club team in Europe, probably the world. Only Rangers will argue with this. They have called themselves the best team in the world since 1873.

The rivalry between them betrays the fierce religious differences. There are no Catholics in the Rangers team. Celtic have three or four Protestants, but that is perhaps because there aren't enough good Catholic players around.

Celtic fly the Irish republican flag over their ground. The club colour is the green of old Ireland. The motif on the club badge is a shamrock. There is a picture of President Kennedy on the manager's wall.

Celtic even have their own religious martyr, John Thomson, the goal-keeper killed in a match against Rangers in 1931. The fans still talk about him as if he died yesterday.

Rangers supporters express their anti-Irish feelings in unexpected ways. Outside Rangers ground last week I could hear kids in the street singing the National Anthem, as if it were a pop song. Rangers fans have now taken it up as a club chant. They have also taken up the Union Jack as their flag. Normally you wouldn't catch Scotsmen dead with this symbol of English oppression, but Rangers fans wave it purely to antagonise the Irish Celtic. Union Jacks are amongst the things banned from Celtic's ground for any Rangers-Celtic match, because of the danger of 'inciting fans to violence'.

Religion is a cause of a lot of the fights, but most people think it is simply the excuse. The hooligan element is going to look for a fight anyway. The truth is that football is the religion, with Rangers and Celtic as the two rival beliefs.

Rangers is the established Church. Their ground, Ibrox Park, is like a cathedral, with a huge marble entrance hall and triumphal staircase leading up to their trophy room. This is their pride and joy, the door is opened with nervous excitement, and you have to admire with hushed breath. They say they have more trophies than any other club in the world and they are the only club which has to set aside a special state room for their proper display.

Rangers have the bigger number of followers, probably the biggest of any club in the world. They even have 200 fan clubs *outside* Glasgow. Rangers supporters' clubs in Detroit, Toronto and Chicago have each got a special charter plane coming for their European final.

The most important man in Glasgow is not the Lord Provost but the chairman of Rangers, a point conceded by the last Lord Provost himself. The present chairman is Mr John Lawrence, a millionaire builder of 73, who is said to have paid £250,000 for his stake in the club. Rangers is unusual in that its shares are public. The highest it has been worth recently on the Stock Exchange is £3 million.

His office at his building firm in Glasgow is a reproduction of the Head

Master of Eton's study. 'I didn't go to Eton myself, though I haven't done bad for a working boy, have I?'

Celtic, on the other hand, have that un-Established, underprivileged air. Their stadium is rather scruffy and unimpressive. I knocked at the front door and the manager popped his head through a hatch. (At Rangers it had taken two trips and several hours before I was eventually led into the manager's presence.)

Jock Stein, Celtic's manager, can afford to dispense with the show. He is by far and away the most successful manager in present-day British football. In two years he has ended Rangers' stranglehold on Scottish awards, provided the best part of the successful Scotland team and got Celtic to the top in Europe. He has bought only two players in that time, keeping Celtic the cheapest top team in Britain.

The biggest irony is that Mr Stein is a Protestant, the first non-Catholic manager Celtic has ever had. 'Celtic,' he says, 'was founded by Catholics and I hope we'll always be proud of our origins, but I'm not interested in a footballer's religion, just his ability and his willingness.'

With such success, it's not too hard for Mr Stein to be so sensible and moderate. Success even brought out a few jokes, something not normally associated with football managers. We were looking at all the green motifs at Celtic's ground – green paint, green badges, green ornaments – when Mr Stein looked at the pitch and smiled. 'Rangers are all right, but they still haven't invented blue grass.'

That was the only smile in the week. Football, like religion, is deadly serious, even in death. An ex-Rangers footballer called Arthur Dixon died a few months ago. His last wish was that his ashes should end up on the pitch at Ibrox. They've just been ceremonially scattered. The turf hasn't turned blue but at least it could now be said to be holy as well as Protestant.

1968

New Kidd on the Block

THE BOY WONDER of the new football season is Brian Kidd. Instant fame settled on him even before the League programme opened in two excellent matches for Manchester United, one of them against Spurs. Now he's already a household name, at least in the North.

There's a Boy Wonder every season, of course. Manchester United's last one was George Best. Mr Kidd is very different and perhaps he'll be the first of the new-style, old-style footballer. His worry is how to avoid the temptations of the flesh.

In just a few short weeks of fame, he's been on Granada TV, been asked by a literary agent to 'write' books, been pointed out in the street and been invited to lots of parties.

'I've had many invitations to parties down town. I could easily get in with all the models and the top people. But why should I? Them sort of people are all false, aren't they? But I still go down to the Knitting Mill where me Mam used to work, just for a chat. They were always nice to me as a kid when I went to pick up me Mam's outdoor work.'

Brian is 18 and knows that top people are false because his Dad has told him. His Dad is a bus driver for Manchester Corporation.

He's been on Manchester United's books since he left his Roman Catholic secondary modern school in Manchester at 15. Since then his Dad has instilled into him the need for self-discipline.

'I have wanted now and again to stay out late, but then me Dad has just pointed out what it would mean. I do go dancing on a Saturday. I feel a bit of a Charlie ordering a Pepsi when all the lads have got pint pots. I can hear them thinking, "Aye, aye, what's he?" I might pick up a girl, but I just see her to her bus. Nothing flash.

'After that Spurs match, I didn't go out at all. I just sat in on me own, watching telly. Me Mam and Dad went out for a drink. I let them in when they came home and I stood at the doorway looking out at the stars. I suddenly felt funny, and sort of great. Me, playing for Manchester United.'

This time last year he was cleaning Denis Law's boots. That was one of his jobs, apart from cleaning down the dressing-room walls. But he'd also graduated to the reserve team, finishing the season as their highest scorer.

During the summer, on United's American and Australian tour, he also met his hero, Eusebio.

'It was in Los Angeles when we were playing Benfica. I was the substitute that day. I was in the same room as him. I just looked at him. I was too shy to express anything.'

He keeps Eusebio's autograph along with his other prized possessions, locked in his mother's china cabinet in the front room of their council house in Moston, Manchester. He sent his younger sister to the secret hiding place where the key is kept. Then he opened the cabinet and brought out a plastic bag which said 'Selected Potatoes'. Inside was a dirty white shirt, very carefully folded.

'This is the shirt I wore when I first played for England's youth team. I've got eight in all. None of them are going to get washed. I want to keep them for ever as they are. Look, see this bloodstain. That's where I got me nose hurt against Scotland.'

Before each match he always says his prayers. Then, when the ref blows the whistle for the off, he crosses himself. 'But if I have a bad game, then I don't blame God. Nobody's infallible. Why should I always have all the luck?

'I have had a lot. It's still a dream, with a 50,000 crowd shouting and actually playing with Denis, Bobby and Georgie.

'When I get depressed or I'm worrying that I might have hurt me ankle, I just think about all the blind people and cripples. They can't run around, never mind play for Manchester United's first team, can they?'

He hasn't been completely unchanged by success. He had six hours to spare on the plane back from the summer tour and read a book, the first time he'd ever read one. It was *No Mean City* about the Gorbals.

He thinks he might read another book some day, but not this season. 'I've got all the football magazines, to read, haven't I?'

He's now in the £100-a-week class, but he's keeping all his money safely in the bank. 'I'd like to buy me Dad a little business. After that I might buy a Jag. But when I have the money. Not H.P. I like the idea of a Jag. That's what the other first teamers have.'

He has no intention of leaving home, not till he gets married. 'Get a flat on me own? You're joking. With me Dad? He'd give me a right shouting-out, a proper sherricking.'

1970

Russian Around

I PLAY for the *Sunday Times* football team and our season ended last week with a little local friendly match against the Russians. To get myself in trim I'd only practised for a whole year, playing Sunday mornings and training on Thursdays. The week before I'd only given up sugar, bread, potatoes and sex, substituting instead a daily cross country, cold showers and *Scouting for Boys*. The day before the match I couldn't sleep. I felt sick. I spent my pre-match lunch alone, locked in my room because my children's whispering was making me a nervous wreck.

It's amazing that I've given the whole of the year to football. During the previous decade, I never kicked a ball, although I was still a fanatic in my head, reading every report about Spurs, my London team, Carlisle United where I was brought up, and Glasgow Rangers, the team of my birth. I suppose I thought that reaching 30 was so unforgivable that I must never bare my knees in public again.

Yet as a kid, like millions of others, I lived for football. Playing all day in the street and all evening under the lamp-posts. In bad weather I played indoors with a rubber ball on a string, practising overhead kicks.

The tensest time, only equalled by our match against the Russians which I'm going to tell you about in a minute if you'll hold on, was when Scotland played England on the radio. That's where they played – on the radio. Wembley and Hampden were fictional places. It was just me, on my own, my head down glued to the set, my heart pounding, living every kick. A metabolic change must have taken place over the years. I find it impossible to follow a match on the radio today.

At 11 when I went to my secondary modern school, I told the headmaster that I wanted to be a professional footballer. I was dead thin and weedy at the time, crippled with asthma, but in my head I was as big and brave as Billy Houliston.

Last year, at 34, it all suddenly started again. I was with my kids and a plastic ball on the Heath and so was another old bloke of 34. I thought I'd show him a few tricks that scored so many goals for Kingstown Rovers in the Carlisle and District Under Sixteen Christian Welfare League, back in the days when football boots were made of lead and you wore two pairs of shorts in case any soppy girls saw you changing on the touchline.

The next week we got a few more good 'uns but old 'uns and it's gone on from there, every Sunday morning on the Heath. The age range is from ten to 50 and we always get enough to pick two full teams.

It's just coats on the ground and the parkies chase us at least once a month for doing something wrong. But the enthusiasm is phenomenal, mainly from the 30s to 40s.

Michael Parkinson is always going on about the gear his kids wear today, compared with his day. He should see us dads. We spend hours discussing studs, ankle pads, jock straps, white or black boots, diets, exercises and we boast like mad about how many games we've played during the previous week. At one time, by hunting around, I was managing six a week.

They're all sorts in our team, all accents and all colours and I've no idea what most of them do during the week. They haven't an idea what I do. As I can always play, any time, I'm assumed to be a burglar. We rarely play against other teams but just pick sides among ourselves, arguing and sulking like primary school kids. I did arrange a *real* match once, with real goal posts, against a Granada TV team. I arranged it, knowing I'd be bound to pick myself, but the eleven regulars who didn't get a game wouldn't speak to me for weeks.

It's a funny mixture of realism and fantasy. If I'm on the losing side, my whole weekend is ruined. My family's life has had to be rearranged. The country cottage we've been looking for for ten years has now had it. I've got to stay in London for the fitba, haven't I?

The fantasy is in thinking I'm really good, which we all do, as we beat ten-year-olds by knocking them over, or by scoring from impossible angles by arguing that the goal coats were wider than they are. I keep thinking that people watching me are thinking, yes, he's not bad, considering his age. He must have been good at 15.

It's probably all some sort of compensation or sublimation. We must all be worried about our virility. Professional footballers keep off sex the night before in case it ruins their football. We dads have taken up football in case we ruin our sex. It's a last desperate fling to show how masculine and tough we are before real middle age sets in.

And so to the match of the decade, The *Sunday Times* against the Russian Embassy. They'd hammered the daily *Times* 8–3 and we'd heard terrible stories about them all being KGB heavies. We met at the Embassy in Kensington Park Gardens (Millionaires Row) last Sunday afternoon. The back garden had been concreted-in as a volleyball court which frightened me. They must train day and night.

The pitch was a delight, the poshest I've ever played on. It's a royal pitch, behind the Embassy, with real nets, real flags, a referee and linesmen in black, oranges at half time and they gave our captain a pennant before the start, a present from the Communist Youth Party. In the dressing-room was a picture of Chivers and a slogan saying 10 + 1= Work rate.

That famous amateur footballer Brian Glanville told us to come on strong

H. Davies, star of the Sunday Times *team against the Russian Embassy, gets attention to his fevered brow, 1970*

for the first five minutes to upset them. 'I know these continental teams.' We did go strong for the whole of the first half and scored two goals, the first from our inside right (I thought you'd never ask). But in the second half, most of us began to show our age, especially me. We won in the end, 2:1.

Afterwards, the *Sunday Times* wives and families were all in their gear and hot pants while the Russians, who'd looked such giants on the pitch, seemed lost in their old-fashioned suits. 'I like to see the hot pants,' said the full back who'd been killing me. 'We don't allow them for normal receptions.'

He said he was a third secretary and his sport was fencing, not football. Then came all the excuses, with the Russian dads trying to better the English dads. It had been their May Day celebrations the day before and they'd been drunk all day. A likely excuse.

Did he realise I was 35 and had a decade without playing? 'You should have seen me at 15,' I was saying, but he was off, looking for hot pants.

1971

The Other Mr Best

CLYDE BEST lives in a council house in the East End of London with the curtains pulled, no car, no telephone. Walking up the overgrown garden you wouldn't believe he was a professional footballer with a First Division football club – not these days, anyway – when they're all supposed to live like pop stars. Clyde Best is black. He's the only black team footballer in the whole First Division. As he's unique, he can only be typical of himself.

Sorry, he said, his wet-look shoe in the door. Could he just do the chatting in our car? Right, then wait outside a minute. He was finishing his lunch. It smelled spicy and chickeny, but the door closed and we got no more clues.

We chatted in the car and then drove him to Ashburton County Secondary School. Clyde, along with the majority of West Ham's professionals, makes an extra pittance by coaching school kids for a few pounds an afternoon. His major pittance from West Ham must be about £100 a week, though, like all footballers, he's not allowed to reveal the exact sum. Only the big stars of West Ham, like Bobby Moore and Geoff Hurst, don't do the extra afternoon work.

'The boys don't appreciate it, I'm afraid,' said Mr Taylor, the PE master. 'The first-years are a bit agog, but the older ones just take Clyde for granted.'

In the corner of the PE master's changing room, Clyde was combing his hair furiously with what looked like a garden fork. It was about six inches long with five dangerous looking steel prongs. He was tearing it through his hair and seemed about to do himself a terrible injury. Bobby Howe says Clyde has two combs, one in wood and one in steel, which the players are always teasing him about. He recently bought himself a huge maxi coat. The first day he had it on, Brian Dear asked him if he'd had to get one to carry his comb in.

Bobby Howe is Clyde's regular team-mate at West Ham. They always room together when they play away. Ron Greenwood, the manager, suggested they should, knowing that an intelligent player like Bobby Howe would be good for a young inexperienced lad newly arrived and feeling very strange in a foreign country.

'He's still shy. He doesn't say much and sometimes he's a bit indistinct – at least, I've seen coaches not understand what he's said, although all his friends do. He's great when we're away because he's so easy going. He'll go along with any suggestions. His favourite phrase is "Makes no difference".'

On the way back to his digs, Clyde admitted under cross-examination that he was born in Bermuda on 24 February 1951. So much for the rumours amongst some fans that he doesn't know his age. His father is a prison warder and he has five sisters and two brothers. He went to the local village school in Somerset, Bermuda, and all he remembers is playing football and cricket. He didn't do much learning at school and now regrets it. His ambition was to become a footballer or cricketer. 'I didn't care which one it would be. I just waited to see who was the first person to approach me.'

He played football for Bermuda at 16 in the World Cup preliminary matches and toured in the USA and South America, but nobody there made him an offer and he came back to play in Bermuda, for Somerset, as an amateur. (There are no professional teams in Bermuda – a crowd of 2,000 is about the biggest they get.) He knew a bit about English League football from watching year-old football matches on television.

He admired Manchester United and Bobby Charlton. 'Then out of the blue, West Ham sent me my air fare, single, to come to London and have a trial.'

Well, it obviously wasn't out of the blue. An Englishman called Graham Adams, national coach for the Bermudan team, had written to a friend back home in English football, Ron Greenwood.

'I don't know why Graham Adams particularly picked on me,' says Ron Greenwood. 'I hadn't heard from him before, or since. I'd met him when I was an instructor at Lilleshall and he was learning. I suppose I'd been friendly to him, as I am to everyone, because there is never any need not to be friendly, and he'd thought of me when he discovered Clyde. His letter describing him was so strong, saying how much Clyde needed to get away in order to develop. He sounded a big strong boy. I thought I'd give him a chance.'

On a rainy Sunday in August 1968, Clyde Best, aged 17 and not long out of school, arrived at London Airport for the first time. There was nobody there to meet him. He felt lost and depressed. 'If I'd had a return fare I would have caught the next plane home.'

He took the airport bus to the terminal and got on a tube to West Ham where he got off and wandered into the night, looking for the football ground. It wasn't long before he was told he'd got off at the wrong station. He should have stayed on for Upton Park.

A man in the street said there would be nobody there at this time of night. So he led him to a council house in nearby Ronald Avenue – the house where Clyde now lives – saying that another coloured West Ham player lived there. They could perhaps help him. Mrs Charles, the lady of the house, did help him, taking him in for the night.

The next day Clyde turned up at West Ham's ground. It wasn't the size of the stadium, nor the dressing-rooms, nor the famous players which impressed him most. His chief memory is of being bowled over by the fact that the club had its own transit van to take the players up to the practice ground at Chadwell Heath.

'Yes, I was very sorry about that mix-up when he arrived, poor lad,' says Mr Greenwood. 'I would have felt like going home myself. We'd sent him a telex to come on Monday but he didn't get it. Funnily enough we were travelling back from Newcastle on that Sunday and my chairman asked me on the train about an agency story saying a Bermudan boy was coming that day for a trial. I said they've got it all wrong, as usual. You can't trust newspapers. He's coming *tomorrow*, Monday. We wouldn't have anyone arriving on a Sunday, would we?'

Back at his digs, Clyde was greeted by his landlady, Mrs Charles, who said his tea was ready for him. Her son Clive Charles was already having his tea. Clyde was smiling for the first time, relaxing more, now that he was at home.

Clyde had a spell in a local hotel when he first arrived. 'It was full of lorry drivers. I never had much to say to them.' He's obviously much happier now he's come to live in Mrs Charles's house, especially as Clive Charles also plays for West Ham, in the reserves.

Mrs Charles is white but her second husband wasn't. He came from Grenada. 'I've got coloured kids as well as white kids and to me they're all the same. I can't tell the difference.' Clive's elder brother John also plays for West Ham – after a period in the first team he is now back in the reserves. But Clive, at 19 just a few months younger than Clyde, is expected eventually to become a first team regular.

Clive was born and brought up in West Ham. He's broad cockney, extrovert and friendly, sharp, witty, a flash dresser. He's Clyde's best friend, although you might not guess it the way he teases Clyde for being a hick from the country, the slow one, the one who gets his slang all wrong, who gets left behind. Except when it comes to playing football. On the field, Clyde is the winner so far.

Clive was at the ground that day when Clyde played his first trial match for the youth team. 'He was fantastic. He could do things we'd never think of trying. He had about 500 shots at goal in a quarter of an hour, hitting everything, at every height. We still talk about it. We'd been taught to lay it off, unless we were right in front of goal. He did the unexpected all the time.'

Clyde himself found it very strange, being expected to play as part of a team, not as an individual who could run all over the pitch and do everything, which he'd done in Bermuda. 'I found it very hard to fit in. I seemed to get stick all the time.'

'I remember that first trial very well,' says Mr Greenwood. 'Clyde was a bit upset by tackling from behind and the speed of tackling generally, but his talent was obvious. He was with the youth team under John Lyall and I left the first team to watch him. They were doing a simple movement, first time volleys at goal. A ball came to him that just wasn't playable first time and it needed a body adjustment and I was sure he was going to miss. He sensed what was needed and without pausing he caught the ball on the knee and in the same movement whacked it into the net. A lesser player could never have done it.

'He's a good pupil, which is very important considering how much he's had to learn. He played his first match in the reserves in snow – the first time he'd ever seen snow and ice. Bobby Moore had come back to help in the reserves that day and we made quite a thing of it, introducing Clyde to the West Ham fans. But he didn't do well that first time on those conditions and was caught now and again off balance.

'But he's learning all the time. He's an exceptional player. He's got natural body movements and fantastic agility. His ability to screen the ball and sweep past a player at the same time is exceptional.

'I'll never forget the way he swept past Dunne at Manchester United, not letting him get near the ball, then laying on a pass for Geoff Hurst to score a great goal. Nor last season against Stoke, when he did a similar movement to that one in his first trial match, bringing the ball down with his knee. It was in the first minute and he swept the ball past Banks into the net in one movement. "God, who's this?" said Banksy.

'I remember that time at Old Trafford,' says Clyde. 'There was a crowd of 58,000 and I just stared at them and thought, "I'm looking at the whole population of Bermuda".'

There was a knock at the back door and in came a man in an old raincoat who looked as if he'd come to read the meter. It was Wally St Pier, West Ham's chief coach, and he'd popped in for a cup of tea. Mrs Charles jumped up, despite her crutches which she uses since an operation on her hip, but Wally said he would get it. He gave her a kiss. 'She's one of the nicest women I've met in my whole life. I discovered her two boys.'

'What a laugh that was,' said Mrs Charles. 'One of my daughters was in when he first came to the door asking for the boys. He said he was a chief scout and he'd call back. We all got ready, waiting for him to turn up in his shorts and his woggle. We thought he said boy scout!'

Thanks to Wally getting in first and scooping up the Charles boys, West Ham seem to have more coloured players on their books than any other team. At the moment they have four full professionals and six schoolboys on the way up through the ranks, two of whom Greenwood says are 'absolutely outstanding'. Not that Mr Greenwood is aware of their colour.

'All I know is I've got four good professionals. I never think of them as coloured.'

'In the London area there is a great wealth of talent amongst the immigrant population and in the very near future it's going to be seen at all levels in football. I don't know why it hasn't happened earlier. Perhaps we've had to wait for the second generation to become teenagers. The first generation immigrants for some reason are not very interested in football. It's a fact. You just have to look at any football crowd in the country and you see very few coloured people. But their children have natural body movements and when they discover football at school they love it.'

Perhaps the weather and heavy grounds don't suit coloured players? 'I do prefer the summer,' says Clyde. 'But if you're a professional, you've got to get used to all sorts of grounds. If you're a forward, it's often easier to get round a back when the ground is muddy.'

Clive says that if you're born here it makes no difference. You're used to the weather. He thinks one reason is that a lot of the young coloured kids are still not as interested in football as white kids. 'At the school where I do the coaching there's a Pakistani player who's really good, but he can't be bothered. He'd rather stay with his own Pakistani friends than mix with the white kids. They're not interested in football, so he doesn't care.

'When you've been brought up in a hot country it's much harder of course,' said Clive. 'Look at Clyde. He's so dozy.'

'Watch it.'

'No, really, I have noticed. These people from right hot countries, they aren't half slow. It drives me mad just going out with Clyde. He walks at half pace. There was four of us the other day, me and him and two girls, and we were tripping over his legs, he was walking that slow. And he's never on time. God, the times I've waited for him.'

'Well,' said Clyde smiling. 'It's all this hustle and bustle. I don't like that.'

Clyde doesn't drink and he was very upset by all the publicity over the Blackpool incident, when four West Ham players – Clyde, Bobby Moore, Jimmy Greaves and Brian Dear – were fined for being out late at a club the night before a match. It was generally accepted that he'd followed the others, being so young, but it was also generally accepted that he must have been drinking as well.

'He was really miserable for weeks,' said Mrs Charles. 'He worried most about what his parents would think back home. It was a big story there of course. Jimmy Greaves himself agreed that Clyde hadn't been drinking so I wrote personally to his mother and told her so. It had been one mistake which he'd regretted and he's learned by it and it's now all forgotten. Coloured parents are much more strict, you know, than other people. Clyde wouldn't go out for weeks afterwards.'

'People are just dying to write to the club and report you,' said Clive. 'And it's always the ones who are on at you the minute you go in a bar and want you to have a drink. You've got to refuse or you'd be drunk in half an hour.'

Clyde might not spend anything on drinks but he lashes out each month on clothes. 'I spend at least £60 on a Friday when the monthly cheque comes through, usually more like £100. Just shirts, shoes, odd things.'

'He's tight, though,' said Clive. 'Never pays his bets. We had a five mile race for £5 and he cracked up at two and wouldn't pay. And what about the fiver on beating Leeds? I gave her mine but we never saw yours.'

'Don't believe him.'

'Hey Clyde, fancy going for a pie and mash?'

'You two are not going out,' said Mrs Charles. 'You've just had your teas anyway. All they do is eat.'

'Give over. I've warned you what we'll do if you keep on at us. We'll get a big house together like the other Besty, won't we, Clyde? We'll have a couple of Swedish au pairs to look after us, and you can just come in during the day to cook for us. Don't say we haven't warned you.'

'What about this week's letter, Clyde?' said Mrs Charles.

'Oh Gawd,' said Clive. 'The first night it happened we was just sitting here and he suddenly started staring at me, really staring. I thought he was having a fit. Then he said "How do you spell 'does'?" He was writing to his mum. You should see his writing. Really poor.'

'Take no notice. I'm not that bad. I have a dictionary by me every time. No use asking him. This summer I'm going back to school. Just for lessons. Not to pass any exams. The Players' Union organise part-time classes for players. I think it's them.'

'It's free. That's why he's going,' said Clive.

'No it isn't. I want to learn. I missed everything at school. I want to do these lessons.'

If they lose on a Saturday, Clyde is the one who is upset most and takes longest to get over it. 'He makes our life miserable as well,' said Mrs Charles. 'He won't talk, apart from yes and no and please and thank you.'

'Oh he's very polite,' said Clive. 'No, seriously, he is. It's not that I haven't got no manners. It's just that he's got a lot more than me. He always says thank you very much after a meal, which I don't. And when he comes down it's always Good morning, Mrs Charles. He's shy, but he's very polite.'

'I'm not shy,' said Clyde. 'I'm just quiet. I don't see any point in talking unless you've something to say.'

Shy or quiet, they all agree Clyde has developed a lot since he arrived, but not drastically. He still feels out of most things, despite being famous locally and getting his share of fan letters and autograph hunters.

'I still look at people and I don't know how to approach them, so people think I'm shy. I don't know what you say, what the rules are. I'd never go up to a girl in a club for fear of upsetting her, although at home I would because that's what you do. Everyone is friendly, even if you don't know them.'

Bobby Howe says he's noticed a big difference. 'He's come out of his shell a lot this season, giving as good as he gets when the lads have a go at him. Someone said they'd seen him out with a white girl and Clyde said, quick as a flash, "I'm not prejudiced".'

Clyde himself is quite sure he has a long future ahead of him. 'I hate being substitute but I look at the ones playing and I think, I can wait. I'll still be here when they've gone.'

He has no idea what he'll do when his playing days are over, but he wouldn't stay in football. 'I wouldn't let a son of mine be a footballer. I'd give him a clip round the ear if he tried.' Clive laughed, knowing Clyde was putting on the accent for his benefit. 'No, there's too much pressure in football. It would send you round the bend. If you lose, no one wants to know you.'

But most people at West Ham think that he could become English football's first black hero, which would encourage a lot of immigrant parents to let their sons be footballers. At the moment they discourage them if anything, preferring them to get a secure job. An English Pele would bring them running. It could happen. After all, Clyde has come a long way in only two full seasons.

'His only problem is that he's a very gentle lad,' says Mr Greenwood. 'You don't have to be rough or tough to be a footballer but when you've got someone as big and well built as he is, the opposition try to get you so you just have to stick up for yourself.

'Look how long it took Martin Chivers to get the confidence he's got now. With Clyde's size and weight he should be able to brush everyone aside, perfectly fairly. But aggression is not in his nature, at the moment. But he's only 20. It'll come.'

1971

Travelling with Spurs

ON THE day of the match against Chelsea, Bill Nicholson comes through his front door looking like a foreman on his day off. He wears a dark sober tie, a dark sober suit and a sparkling white shirt. He gets into his car, a white Rover 2000, and his image begins to alter.

In the dressing-room with Spurs, 1972: Bill Nicholson, Manager, with Ralph Coates, Mike England, Terry Naylor and Alan Gilzean

The manager takes over from the foreman – a manager going off to manage a group of people he has personally spent £1 million on creating.

It is raining in White Hart Lane and they are rushing from their sports cars into the coach, dashing past Eddie Baily, Nicholson's assistant, who is ticking them off on his list. Inside the manager's office, Nicholson glances at his post and makes a few phone calls, staring at nothing, showing no emotion.

The team on the coach are resplendent in their best leather coats, long collars, kipper ties, wet look shoes and expensive hair. One of the jobs which Nicholson did during the winter of 1936, his first year as a boy on the ground staff with Spurs, was painting the roofs of the grandstands from eight to five. 'I rarely had a jacket on at all. I think the South must have softened me over the years.'

In the coach, they are shouting under their breath, waiting for him to hurry up. The car park and the stadium are deserted. The modern, fully equipped gymnasium and the indoor ball court, almost the size of a football pitch, are empty. When Bill Nicholson was a young player with Spurs he remembers training on gravel with a cloth ball full of straw.

At 51, Nicholson has the ageless looks he must have had as a player, 20 years ago. He spent one year after school on a drying machine in a laundry in his home town of Scarborough. Apart from that, he has devoted a lifetime to Tottenham Hotspur Football Club.

He never expected to be manager. He'd stayed on after his playing days as a coach, mastering all the new developments. 'I came in one morning in October, 1958, and the chairman asked to see me. I had no idea what he wanted. He told me the manager was resigning and he wanted me to take over.'

They never got round to signing a contract, and Nicholson decided it was unnecessary. Success is the contract. 'Tottenham is one of the senior clubs with tremendous facilities and enormous status. Anything less than top class would not be accepted at Spurs. I would expect to get the sack,' he says, 'if Spurs were not successful.'

Nicholson is a dour, controlled, apparently cold personality. Yet he has constantly striven for lightness and brightness, for excitement and skills and, above all, for entertainment. In an era of defence, he has dreamt only of attack. In his first five years Spurs won the FA Cup twice, the Football League and the European Cup Winners Cup.

Eddie Baily gives them a final count, checking that Mullery, Beal and Perryman are definitely making their own way.

As the coach turns into Tottenham High Road Johnny Wallis, the trainer, asks Nicholson if he's heard about the accident in the road last night. The two of them are alone at the front of the bus, stranded like base-camp survivors with the bags and baggage, comparing road accidents. Isolated in the middle of the long coach is a lady from the club, Mrs Barbara Wallace, who works in the front office. She is in her best outfit, like everyone on the bus, and wears a silver brooch in the shape of a cockerel, the Spurs emblem, on her lapel. Beside her is a man in a suede coat called Basil. He is a travel agent: the only fan allowed to travel anywhere near the team.

Some London clubs have more hangers-on than players – usually people from the rag trade or minor show business stars. You have to get in with Bill Nicholson to get in with Spurs. Getting in with Bill Nicholson is like getting in with Greta Garbo.

At the back of the coach are the team. Only Alan Gilzean, the oldest Spurs' player, looks slightly out of place in a two-piece dark suit, stuck amongst the pop stars, when he should be with the two roadies at the front of the bus. He is sitting alone, staring out of the window, muttering. He is tall and distinguished, with a high dome and receding hair. Coming close, it's a surprise to hear him cursing in a broad Scottish accent.

The players talk about last night's TV, or half-mockingly admire each other's clothes. No one talks about where they are going. Today is going to be a vital match. Not just because it is a derby match, against old enemies – but because the outcome will decide which of them stays in the top three League positions.

Chelsea have not even been mentioned during the week's routine training. 'We worry about ourselves in this club, not the opposition,' says Nicholson. 'All our tactics are worked out before the season begins. What we do in training is brush-up on things that aren't going right.

'In patches, we were bloody awful last Saturday.' (They beat Burnley 4–0.) 'When we play well, we're brilliant entertainers. Other times we can be awful. I can't understand it.'

Cheshunt, nine miles up the Cambridge road from Tottenham, is where Spurs try to understand themselves in their morning training sessions. The first team, under Bill Nicholson, train in red shirts. They look famous and confident and very adult. The reserves, dressed in blue, are under Eddie Baily. They look solid and workmanlike, but a little sullen and spotty-faced. The youth team, under Pat Welton, look somehow old-fashioned, with shirts hanging out and over-large shorts bagging round their thin, teenage legs. The first team are all thigh.

'The difference between a good player and a bad player,' says Eddie Baily, 'is like the difference between failure and success. It's that much.' He holds up a finger and thumb. The gap of air between is scarcely perceptible.

'Training is vital,' says Nicholson, 'repeating and repeating every possible action. Look at tennis players. You see them serving the same ball, over and over again. Footballers have got to do the same.

'If you don't practise, you get rusty. I can prove it. I can suddenly test a certain skill, like trapping the ball, for example. You can see the first attempts. After half an hour's practice the difference is so marked that anyone can see it.'

Nicholson starts his players training two at a time, kicking the ball awkwardly in the air for the other to trap. Gently, he encourages or reprimands them. On the other pitches, the other two coaches are screaming like sergeant-majors, working themselves into a lather of orders and abuse. Some of their players argue back, defending themselves when they're screamed at."

On the first-team pitch, no one argues with Mr Nicholson. But still, nobody likes exercises; it's the practice match they like best.

'Gilly, what are you doing?' shouts Nicholson at Alan Gilzean. Gilzean has expertly trapped the ball in Brazilian fashion by bringing it down on the end of his toe. 'Trap it under your foot, or with your instep,' demands Nicholson. 'It's all very well doing it that way, but what happens in wet weather?'

After training, one or two players have cuts attended to by Johnny Wallis, the trainer. They stand around like ballerinas, with one foot up on the bench, staring out at the youth team sitting outside, raggedly and exhausted, waiting for the first team to finish with the dressing-room.

'You've not got to be hard on Dainsey,' says Hancock, the reserve goalkeeper, to Baily. 'You've got to be tender.'

'Tender! Christ Almighty,' says Baily, looking round, half joking. 'At his age, I had a bloody rifle stuck in my hand.'

London could hardly be wetter, for trapping or travelling, as the Chelsea-bound coach draws out of Great Portland Street towards Harley Street. 'Hey, Martin,' someone shouts to Martin Chivers, 'there's your place.'

'Yes, that's the window,' says Chivers pointing up at the Royal Orthopaedic Hospital, visited at some time by many London footballers when they have a leg injury. Last season, Chivers was out of football ten months with a knee injury.

'The fear of breaking a leg is always with you,' says Gilzean. 'Footballers are lying who say it never worries them. In a match you do forget and hurl yourself into tackles, but sometime during the week it comes into your head that it might happen this Saturday. It's very hard to get over an injury. The doctor says okay, it's better now, but it's very difficult to stop carrying it.'

When Joe Kinnear, the young full-back, broke his leg he was out of football for 12 months. His mother couldn't sleep for worry: she lost three-and-a-half stone in the year. Joe thought it was the end. 'I can hardly believe it now that in that year nobody came out of the cheque book to fill my place.'

All the Spurs players who work their way up internally, starting with the club as a youth player, have this constant worry that Spurs, because of their resources and reputation, will buy somebody better, or perhaps just more famous, and they'll be out.

'You might be only 19 with a great future but you know if they buy a famous player of 24 in your position you might as well leave. It brings crowds in if a big star is signed.' His mother is always saying it's unfair. 'They're always making allowances for these big new stars. If he doesn't play well they say he's got a headache, but when a youngster who only cost the club £10 plays badly it's Out, Out, Out. . . .'

Kinnear is 23 and a bachelor and he's the player they all think is a bit of a raver, who lives it up. He does look flash arriving for the coach in his red MGB GT, and a few days ago he bought seven shirts at £5 15s each in a boutique in Hampstead. But he lives quietly in Watford with his family.

Martin Peters is the really quiet one. It's all in his head and never comes out except through his feet on the field. He's had to take a lot of jokes since Sir Alf Ramsey said that as a player he was ten years ahead of his time.

More bare facts from the Spurs dressing-room, 1972

Naturally, everybody asks if his £16,000 new house is really new or 10 years ahead of its time. When he got a new car they all said it must be a prototype.

He cost Nicholson £200,000, the costliest footballer in the country. He sits alone on a double seat looking out of the window.

Bill Nicholson comes down the bus with a bundle of what look like labels, as if he is going to stick one round each neck so they won't get lost in the big crowd at Stamford Bridge. He peels off three each. These are the free tickets, the number allowed for each first-team player for each away match. They get out envelopes, put the tickets inside and scrawl friends' names on the front.

Ken Hancock, the reserve goalie, pulls out a packet of sandwiches and begins eating. Everyone else looks disgusted. No one wants to eat. Suddenly, the coach is out on a motorway, and they are wiping the windows, shouting that they are lost. Basil, the travel agent fan, calls out, pointing to Queen's Park Rangers' stadium: they're on the new flyover.

Nicholson, keeping himself to himself, stares out of the front window as if navigating. 'That's how it should be,' says one player nodding towards the front. 'You wouldn't want a manager mucking in – being one of the lads. It would inhibit you, wouldn't it, if you were talking about birds, for instance?

Look at Tommy Docherty. He used to muck in with the players, but when the time came for discipline, it led to animosity.'

The last word hangs in the air, as if the speaker himself is surprised it should come out. Conversation is false and self-conscious: the players are watching each other, but really watching themselves, containing their emotions, putting on the heavy boredom. Someone mentions the Young Generation being on TV. Everyone agrees passively they could play a good game against them.

The streets are crowded now and the coach crawling as they near the Fulham Road. Despite the rain the crowds are streaming towards the ground. Could it possibly be a record crowd on a day like this? The players ignore the outside world, still chattering away, becoming more animated. Nicholson peers out, looking worried, hoping for signs.

He finds it difficult to relax, to take part in idle chat. If he does manage an hour's TV, he will suddenly jump up and say that's another hour he's wasted. He expects his wife Grace to jump to attention when he sounds his horn outside, at whatever time he arrives back, to open the garage doors for him. His wife moans that he would really like a flat on top of the stadium, so that he could always be on the job. They live in White Hart Lane.

It's often after midnight by the time he does get home. The evenings are when he sees other clubs and other players that he or the scouts think he should see. It's not unusual for him to leave the ground after a full day's work, pick up a ticket at London Airport and fly to Scotland for a second division match, coming back overnight. In England he usually drives himself. He'd just been up to Huddersfield in an evening, doing the 186 miles back in three hours.

'There's never any problems about sleep. When I get into bed, I collapse. It's only Saturday nights when I'm so keyed up that I've got to put off going to bed till the early hours as I know I'll never sleep. I'll never sleep tonight.'

At last, among the boys at the back, someone mentions Chelsea. 'I've never been on the winning side here since I joined Spurs in 1964,' says Gilzean. 'There again, Chelsea hasn't beaten us at Tottenham.'

'Luck plays such a part. We're both having a good run at the moment, yet last season at this time we were nowhere. I don't know what does it. Look at how badly Everton are doing, yet they've the same team that won the League last year. Or Wolves. They started off with ten defeats in a row, now look at them. Often you work harder when things are going badly. You're trying to make the break that just won't come. When it does, you get confidence. You've just got to keep fighting.

'Chelsea's a funny ground, with the spectators so far from the park. At Spurs, they're on top of you, so you get a good atmosphere. It's always a big match at Chelsea. Not such a derby as when we play Arsenal. But almost.'

At Chelsea's ground there is a hurried police escort off the coach and a line of guards into the players' entrance, the crowd nudging each other as they recognise a famous face. A few minutes later, several players reappear, alone this time, going personally to deposit their free tickets at the ticket office. As each fights his way through the crowds, no one notices. You wouldn't notice the Queen if she was on the Underground. You wouldn't notice Martin Peters if he was standing in a football crowd.

The visitors' dressing-room at Chelsea is much smaller than Spurs' own dressing-room at home. It's L shaped and rather crowded and the communal bath is more old fashioned.

The Tottenham players arrive with an hour to wait before the kick-off. Their strips and boots are laid out as if for inspection, in order along the bench seats, from goalkeeper round to outside-left. They undress, hanging up their clothes on their pegs. Then they stand around chatting, or sit on the benches while Johnny Wallis puts plasters on any injuries, or ties up their shin pads with strips of plaster. Most have special ankle socks to protect them, taped on under their football socks.

Once they've got their boots on, most of them walk about, delaying as long as possible before putting on their shorts and shirts. They stamp round, some sliding on the floor, awkwardly as if they had high heels. Most of them still have a sun tan left over from the summer. Pat Jennings' flesh is very white, except for the red and blue bruises on his shoulders from the last match.

'I'm off to the library,' says Chivers, still dressed only in his boots. He picks up a programme from the middle table and goes off to the lavatory to read it.

Two reserves in their street clothes are standing against one wall, outsiders, neither daring to take off his coat, Just in case he might be forcing his luck. One reserve will be named as substitute and be told to strip off. The other will have to spend the afternoon in his street clothes, watching. 'Did I tell you about my dream last night?' said one to the other. 'You got picked.'

Bill Nicholson comes in with a list of the Chelsea team changes. He chooses one reserve, then goes round several players, telling them quietly what they will now have to do.

Their little rituals over, the players begin to oil themselves, picking up Johnny Wallis's dark brown bottles full of warm oil. They work the oil into their legs. Alan Gilzean rubs oil all over his chest.

At three minutes to three, the Spurs players go through their final rite. Solemnly and in turn, each player shakes hands with everyone else, ten handshakes, wishing each other good luck, a good game and no injuries. As they go out of the dressing-room and up the corridors to the field, Bill Nicholson touches each on the back. 'Good luck Alan. Good luck Pat. Good luck Joe. . . . '

The rain is torrential. You can see the water lying along the middle of the pitch. Yet both sides play excellent football.

In the first half Spurs have the edge, but in the second half it is all Chelsea, gradually wearing Spurs down and looking all set to score at least one goal for a well deserved win. As usual, Chelsea are storming to a late finish with Charlie Cooke dancing round Spurs' defenders as they stumble in the mud.

Bill Nicholson is bracing himself for a draw.

Then the spirit which looks after football teams decides, perversely, to smile on Spurs. It could only be a spirit, because the interruption comes so late, well after normal time, that no human agency could send it. In two minutes of injury time, Spurs score twice. The first is a Mullery shot on the edge of the penalty area and the second comes from a giant throw by Chivers, going to Gilzean's head and then to Pearce who pushes it in.

The crowd is silenced. The Chelsea team look dazed. They can't believe it. It is so unfair. As Alan Mullery says afterwards, even Chelsea, with their habit of finishing late, couldn't come back in the 92nd minute.

In the press box, the allegedly unbiased press are equally silenced. They have already written their reports in their heads, all about Chelsea's great victory. It's not just that Chelsea is a favoured team – which they are – or that Charlie Cooke is a friend of so many journalists – which he is – but that for the whole second half Spurs have shown absolutely no sign of winning.

In the dressing room, Spurs can hardly be contained. 'Cor,' says Chivers. 'Talk about stealing the crown jewels.' Even Martin Peters normally so quiet and withdrawn is excited. 'Party my place tonight, lads. You know how to get there. Third right, second left. (Pause) Don't worry if I'm not there.'

'Hey,' shouts Chivers from the bath, 'who said it was 50,000? It was over 60,000. Who told me it was 50,000?'

The match has drawn 61,277, the biggest crowd of the season for both teams. In terms of money, it is an all-time record for Chelsea – £24,500.

'It was on your noddle, what do you mean, Mart?' 'You can't dive up,' replies Martin Chivers. 'When you dive you lose height.' 'The puke was in my mouth that time,' says Joe Kinnear. 'Did you speak to Johnstone when he came on as a sub?' asks someone else. 'He was supposed to come on and mark Charlie Cooke. He ended up marking Martin Peters.' They all laugh.

'He said that Bill had a message for each of us but he hadn't got time to give it us.' They laugh even louder. 'We deserved that goal from the throw-in. After practising throw-ins three hours a day it's got to come some time.'

'No, how we really won,' says Joe Kinnear, 'I shouted Shazan and that was it. Didn't you hear me?'

'What about Ossie? Arrogant as usual, wasn't he?'

'Who was it who told me to pick up Webbie?' 'Christ, I could eat an elephant.'

Ken Hancock comes in, an outsider in his clean suit. He hasn't been down the mines with the rest of his mates. He is eating a bundle of sandwiches. 'I was in the directors' box with this posh bird in front of me. You should have seen her face when I jumped up and screamed when you scored. Pardon. I wish they wouldn't put cucumber in these prawn sandwiches.'

'Arsenal's my banker,' says Joe Kinnear as the results come over the radio. 'How did Millwall get on?' asks Martin Peters. 'Did Yo-Yo score?' 'I bet there was a big cheer in the reserves' dressing-room when our score came through.' 'That's another draw I haven't got.' 'Anyone hear Millwall?'

One or two early ones are sitting in the dark in the coach, waiting for the others. 'I wish they'd bloody hurry up,' says Gilzean. 'What about Millwall?' asks Peters.

On a staircase inside the stadium, just outside the directors' bar, Bill Nicholson is hurrying along accompanied by Mrs Wallace. On the top of the steps they run into Dave Sexton, the Chelsea manager. They stop suddenly, both almost guiltily caught in a situation they want to avoid. Nicholson's face is drawn and blotchy, the excitement having brought the red veins to the surface of his face.

Sexton stiffly nods congratulations. He means to say 'well done,' but his jaw opens and he can only mumble and smile a death-mask smile as if he'd been laid out and the mortician has painted it on.

He stands without talking, unable to form words or to erase his death smile or stop his head from nodding. Nicholson on the other hand, the silent, dour Nicholson who never gives anything away, has come to life as if his blood vessels have finally burst. It all blurts out in a torrent which he can't stop.

'I went on the pitch beforehand, Dave, and it was good, really good, the pitch was really good, they'd done a good job and then all the rain came down I don't think I've seen conditions like that for a match before, I really haven't, Dave. . . .'

Suddenly, he stops, and they both moved away. For victor and loser the result has been shattering.

'Watch out for bricks,' says Ken Hancock as the coach crawls through the crowds in the Fulham Road. 'It must have been that new way we came to the ground. Hey, Martin. Your hair looks better after all that rain.'

As they go down Piccadilly, Joe Kinnear says he is going to see Tony Bennett tonight. 'Where's he on at?' asks Mike England earnestly. 'He's not,' says Kinnear. 'He's coming to our house.'

Pat Jennings is sitting silently on the back seat. Blood has congealed on his forehead like stigmata. He collided with a goalpost during the match.

'I think the driver's lost,' says Gilly, still moaning. 'Och aye. I'm pleased enough. But there's a long way to go yet. It's not the end of the road.' All the way home, Bill Nicholson says nothing.

1971

Arsenal Win at Wembley

IMMEDIATELY AFTERWARDS, there was a strange silent atmosphere in the Arsenal dressing-room. Some were still getting washed and others were half dressed, staring into space, slightly numbed. An event in search of an atmosphere. McNab was lying naked on his back on the injury table autographing a programme. They were still moaning about being tired and suffering from cramp.

'I can't grasp it yet,' said Frank McLintock. 'I'm still too involved in the game. I'm not as pleased as I thought I would be. Mind you, it hits you very quickly when you've lost. Winning has to sink in.'

Bertie Mee came round followed by the well-wishers and the dressing-room at last took on a winning noise with reporters crowding round him and policemen scurrying about with programmes getting the players' autographs. Mr Mee spoke slowly and carefully . . . the gentleman manager choosing his grammar with care.

'One is too involved with one's assets and one's efficiency to worry. I think we created chances 6–2 compared with Liverpool. Our finishing wasn't as good as it could have been. We've come from behind before. One recaptures experiences of the past and one says, "Come on, we can do it again." It really all happened in the last four or five weeks. We picked up a team momentum just at the right time and nothing went wrong.' Then suddenly he caught sight of someone he didn't like and momentarily forgot himself. 'I want that gentleman in the maroon suit removed from this dressing-room. I'm sorry. You were asking. How do I feel? This is a factual thing, talking to you, that's all I can say. It's a factual thing . . .' And he finished incoherently.

George Graham was being congratulated on being voted player of the match. 'They're fair judges. I can't disagree, can I? No, don't put that down. I was joking.' Arsenal players are modest at all times.

They were all smiling now, drinking champagne, beer and milk. Charlie George had recovered his cockiness. 'Of course, I didn't expect Liverpool to play any better. Where are they in the League, eh?'

In the Liverpool dressing-room only Hall and Heighway, the country's two famous graduates, had the energy to say very much, and it was the event, not the result, which had impressed them most. All the others were too dejected. Toshack sat in shirt sleeves for almost an hour after the match transfixed to the bench, unable and unwilling to put on his immaculate club blazer.

Smith, the captain, was sitting on a bench while the trainer attended to his feet. On the field he always looks as if he eats razor blades for tea and shaves with a blow lamp. He was sad and miserable, almost in tears, sitting in a very posh pair of orange boxer underpants, not the sort you'd expect Desperate Dan to wear. The trainer had his scissors at the ready, about to snip off chunks of blistered skin, looking up at Smith, worried that he might hurt him. 'Cut it all off,' said Smith, flatly.

Heighway was about the only player in either camp who thought it had been an even game. 'I don't think they proved themselves any better than us. It was a game with three incidents. They scored from two and we scored from one. My goal was the first chance I'd had for a run at Rice without him having any cover. Wilson says it hit the post? He would. He had his slide rule out, I suppose.

'I was more tense than I thought I'd be. I'd prided myself on being very composed. It was Friday night at the Palladium that did it. Anita Harris said there were some stars in the audience and they all cheered. I realised then that it was more than just Liverpool against Arsenal. The Cup Final is more of an event than a General Election. More important as well. It makes life a lot less tedious. We got to Wembley, that's the big thing. They can't take that away.'

Brian Hall thought Arsenal had the edge. 'They had older heads on their side who created more chances, but it will come. We're a new side. I thought we'd won when Steve scored but then they got that scrappy goal. After such a great season our defence had to make a mistake. Their second goal was better but even that hit big Larry on the way.

'I was very tense beforehand. You can't help it. You read about it in the paper all the time. People come up to you in the street and say "You've *got* to win." Up to now I've gone into every match to enjoy it rather than to win it. This time I went in to win. I'd never realised how many people were involved. As we came down the tunnel this poor boy of about 21 was in tears.'

'My wife will be very disappointed. She's eight months pregnant. She hasn't had the fun of being here like me. I enjoyed it all. And I give every credit to Arsenal.'

Getting Mr Shankly to give Arsenal credit, or even let their name soil his lips, was impossible. Had he heard that Mr Mee thought the chances had been 6–2 in Arsenal's favour? 'I'm not interested in talking about Mr Mee. And I'm not interested in talking to you.'

1972

My Son, the Fan

WHEN MY son Jake was born, one of my first thoughts was oh good, someone to go to football matches with. In every Hampstead in every town in Britain there are middle-class, middle-aged dads going on and on in their terribly manly ways about how they and their sons just live for Saturday and the footer match and of course they always stand though actually we missed last week. In fact haven't been this season. I like to think my response was genuine.

One of the regrets of my teenage years was not that we lived in Carlisle, where not many all-time greats greated, but that my dad became an invalid and unable to take me to matches. It was obviously a regret to him as well. He once played, when in the RAF, for Hearts, the Edinburgh club. Boast boast.

I first took Jake to Spurs when he was five and I said never again. He was bored stiff, fidgeted all the time, wanted the lav or drinks every five minutes and thought that every corner was a goal. I took him the next week, and said never again again. He soon got all the gear, of course, like primary school kids everywhere, though in our area mums preferred Arsenal to Spurs as white shirts are a load of trouble and get filthy in minutes.

I should have spotted the first signs. When boring old Arsenal won the double, and every half-witted, fashion-following kid suddenly sported their shirts, Jake was still sleeping in his Spurs top.

His school work has always been unbelievably scruffy, finger marks and smudges everywhere. He doesn't just read books – he attacks them, grinding back the spines so they break instantly, punching them in the face, kicking hell out of their insides. It's a one-sided fight. Jake always wins. You can tell he's read a book by the debris. Wordsworth was much the same, about books I mean. He upset Thomas De Quincey for ever by giving him back a virgin copy of a book with jam stains on every page.

Wordsworth was neat enough when it came to things he cared about, and so, it transpired, was Jake. We discovered in his bedroom a beautifully arranged pile of every Spurs programme I'd ever bought him, in pristine condition, and even more amazing, the most incredibly detailed charts about Spurs' season so far. There wasn't a smudge anywhere.

It's all your fault, she said. Why can't you channel his energies into Latin. You're making one discipline more important than another, I said smugly. There is no intrinsic advantage in learning Latin verbs as opposed to learning

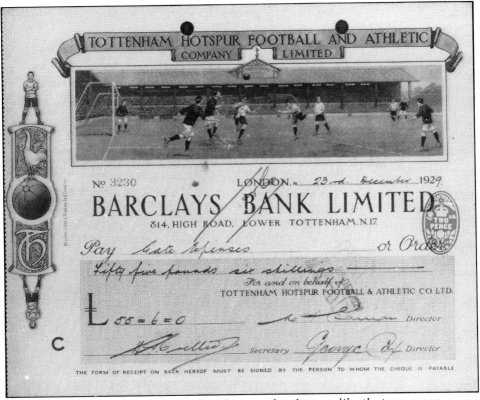

Vignette from 1929: ah, they don't make cheques like that anymore

Spurs' pre-war Cup runs. It's one of the mythologies of traditional education, along with the idea of team games being good for the character. Rubbish, she said. They do Latin at O-level not football results, thank God. Stick around, I said. By the time he's 18, they'll be giving PhDs on Tommy Doc and his middle QPR period.

When we came back from our holiday in Portugal last year, we arrived at Heathrow late in the evening and Jake immediately started grubbing in the debris under some chair and found a torn copy of the *Sunday Express*. . . . Liverpool 7, Spurs 0. I thought he was going to have a heart attack.

The early part of this season has been terrible. Spurs are playing badly and I have to handle him with such care all the way back from matches. He screams and swears when we tune into *Sports Report* and the reporter says Middlesbrough deserved to win 3–1. He's still convinced all those seven Liverpool goals were lucky, when he hadn't even been there, so anyone who dares to report a match he *has* seen and doesn't agree that we was robbed, is a * * * * stupid * * * * and he'll never buy their paper again or listen to their report. And he never does.

I happened to say, one Wednesday evening, how about going to Arsenal as I see they're at home. Watch Arsenal? You must be * * * * joking! Go in disguise, I said, so any school friends won't see you. That was typical of me, making a cheap joke. The point was he would never want to see such a load of * * * *, whether he was spotted there or not. I promised him drinks and goodies at half-time, and I also said I would stand. I prefer sitting down any time, which I always do at Spurs, and, as I'm paying and driving him there and back, he always unwillingly agrees. In his code, only phonies sit. Real supporters stand. I eventually got him to go with me by saying I wanted to see Arsenal *lose*. That surely would be a pleasure. * * * * Arsenal beat Leeds 7–0. He's never going to Highbury ever again.

I've been tarred since then as disloyal. He's brought my own liking for Spurs into serious doubt. I secretly think they've deserved to lose every game I've seen them lose, though I can't say so, not out loud. I'm beginning to think I want to see a good, skilful, exciting game, regardless of the teams. Such abstract discussions are pointless. He's too busy kicking the furniture, banging the doors, doing his Just William scowl. I fear for his wife in years to come and begin to wonder if I've bred a monster. Because I have equivocal thoughts, murmur heretical observations, follow disloyal action, I'm now branded as a traitor. I'm not fit to touch the hem of Chivers's jock-strap.

I've had to tell him the bad news that I probably won't be able to take him to the Forest home game. I'm working on it, but I rashly promised the rest of the family we'd have a day out in the country, probably at my sister's in Leighton Buzzard. I got caught, agreeing without looking up the fixture list. You neglect the rest of the family at weekends anyway, my wife says, with boring old football all the time, so it's about time you thought of us. Jake has taken it like a man. He's decided he'll go on his own. Right across north London, on endless buses and complicated connections, then that huge walk up Tottenham High Road with all the Forest hooligans looking for little lads wearing Spurs scarves. I'm still going, he says. I'm a true supporter. He's never been on his own before. Most lads of his age are hopeless at going places anyway, though when his sister Caitlin was his age she'd practically been in orbit, but then London teenage girls are rather advanced. Last night as I went into his bedroom – well, I have a last look at them all, even now, to make sure they're still alive, and at home – he'd fallen asleep with the light on. Over his face, half in his open mouth as he snored away, was the London bus map.

If he does get thumped, then of course it will all be my fault, having started him on this stupid football fanaticism. If he doesn't get thumped, and manages it all safely, then I know what will happen. He has hardly liked going with me all season as it is, as I moan on about having to drive all the way to places like Crystal Palace, and I often decide not to go at all if the weather's bad. If he manages it, it will be the end of an era. He won't have to come with me anymore, nor will he want to, not now that I've been revealed as just another Hampstead dad. . . .

1972

Clever Clown

RODNEY MARSH is so shyly arrogant, so humbly conceited, that it's not surprising he inspires so much love-hate. He turned up for training and took off his white Lotus Europa like an old glove, letting it lie where it fell. Typical of the bastard, said someone, leaving his car to block the way for everyone else. But they couldn't take their eyes off him, once he started turning it on. Rodney Marsh has star quality, even doing press-ups in the mist in the wilds of Ruislip.

He was knackered at the end, which is the point of training, so that sweat stood out like melting cheese. There's one thing Mr Marsh prides himself on these days: he's a professional, working for the good of the team rather than the good of R. Marsh.

'I came into football to project myself. I wanted the limelight and the glory. At 18 when I was playing for Fulham I saw myself as brilliant as Denis Law, off the field as well as on. I worked on my extrovert image, playing the clown, being a joker.

'Then one day when I was 20 we beat Manchester United and I rushed home to watch it on *Match of the Day*. I saw myself for the first time as a very poor imitation of Denis Law. When I left Fulham six months later for Rangers, I became a different person. I decided to stop being the clown.'

He was now sitting at home, half-serious, half-smiling. The phrases were coming out as if he'd rehearsed them in his head. I said I didn't believe them. He was looking back at himself, rationalising his actions.

'You're right. Nothing's true. Talking to you now I'm acting another part. It's all a façade. Perhaps acting the clown was me and I didn't realise it at the time. All the same, I regret it now, whether I was doing it deliberately or not. I know now what I didn't know then. Managers don't like clowns.'

The transformation has resulted in his being picked for England for the first time, at the great age of 27. He's not only the handsomest, the richest, the most glamorous player in the Second Divison, he's now the most successful. He puts it down to Bobby Campbell, the Queen's Park Rangers' coach.

'It happened about a year ago when Bobby came. I've always been a flash bloke. I thought I knew it all. But Bobby was the first person who got through to me about the need for discipline.'

And now, do people no longer hate you? 'Hold on,' he said, getting up to answer the phone. 'Keep hold of that question, I've got a good answer for you.'

His home is in the heart of stockbroker Epsom where he's realised the Footballer's Dream – blonde wife, a boy Jonathan, a girl Joanna, lovely house, lovely neighbours, lovely life. Not that he's taken in by it all, or by himself. 'Stand back,' he'd said earlier as he was putting his car in the garage. 'I'll put on the suburban coach lamps and give you a treat.'

He finished on the phone, then it rang again. It never stopped. All the world and his agent wants to talk to him. He took it off the hook in the end, by which time he'd forgotten what his smart answer was going to be.

Behind him was a book case, full of books. Boswell's *Life of Johnson, Pears Cyclopaedia.* He waved a hand and said there were more in the next room. A few months ago, so he says, he was thinking of going in for the Open University. 'But what happens if you end up a teacher on £12 to £15 a week? Not much satisfaction there.

'I'll tell you what though, if I hadn't been a footballer I wouldn't have stayed in England. I don't like the English climate and the people are too reserved. I was invited to a party in Epsom the other day. The bloke was on the phone, telling me blah blah what a great party it was going to be, and then he said a couple of special friends were coming who wanted to see me. I never went, of course. That sort of thing happens in England. People want to see me . . . just because I play for Queen's Park Rangers.'

Fractionally, just fractionally, he'd hesitated over the last three words. It looked as if he was going to say 'just because I'm Rodney Marsh' or 'just because I play for England.' But the new Marsh had corrected himself, just in time. Was he ashamed of playing for a Second Division side? Was that why he'd deliberately dragged it in? He refused to be drawn. He was being so well paid, he couldn't leave. He didn't know anything about First Division clubs offering £200,000 for him. Anyway, Rangers would be in the First Division next season.

When his playing days are over, he fancies staying in football, as a manager. Very few footballers say that: they couldn't stand the aggravation – directors, Press, fans, players, all on their backs. 'A manager's aggravation is self-made. I wouldn't find directors or the Press a hardship. All a manager has to do is keep 11 players happy – the 11 in the reserves. The first team are happy, because they're the first team.'

He doesn't intend to sit his FA preliminary coaching badge, the accepted beginning for any player wanting to be a manager. 'No, sir. If I'm going to be a manager, I'm going to be a successful manager. I have most of the football knowledge I need, but I have to learn about management. All football managers are untrained in management. I'll do a business management course at a business college. I'm not bothering with any FA badges.

'Sometimes I think there is something in my life I'm lacking. I can't pin it down. It would take hours and if I boiled it down I know I'd come to the same answer – football for me is the best way out of the crowd. Football has stopped me being ordinary.'

'I don't worry that it's short-lived. I've now got more cynical. I was taken for granted when I was much younger. Now I try to get as much as I can, to do nothing for nothing.

'But what is it, being a footballer? In theory, if you take away Match of the Day and the Press and the fans and the hangers-on, it's all very empty and lonely. When you take it out of context, what is it?'

You mean you'd rather be doing something really creative, like discovering penicillin? 'No, Sir. Alexander Fleming knew that what he was doing was right and good, even if he'd never discovered penicillin. That must be a nice feeling.'

But isn't it nice to think of the pleasure which football gives to millions of people? 'I agree. Football's a great game. But it's being out there that matters most, not talking about it. That's what I like best. You can't cheat, not in football. You can cheat in life, cheat at home, cheat at work. You can talk yourself in and out of anything. I can talk about the great game I'm going to play on Saturday. But I can't out there. I'm out there to be shot at, simply for what I am.'

Mr. GROOMBRIDGE. Mr. CORBETT. Mr. WATSON. CARROLL.
GENTLE. SLAVE. PELLATT. GASCOIGNE. COCKRILL. BRUCE.

Photo by R. Hider. Sheerness.

THOMAS. FRETTINGHAM. HUTCHESON. GLADWELL. PETERS

NEW BROMPTON.

1972

Jimmy, Jimmy

JIMMY HILL is a living, talking, smiling proof that all footballers aren't thick. As chairman of the Professional Footballers Association in 1961 he routed the massed ranks of the football clubs and the Football League and got the £20 maximum wage abolished, a victory which has gone down in trade union history and changed the face of football. As manager of Coventry City, he led them from the Third to the First Division in five years, then suddenly left them. As head of sport at London Weekend TV he's built up a department from scratch which now rivals and sometimes betters the BBC. These are three great achievements, one of which would be enough for normal mortals.

The other day he was standing in the Sportsman Club (helping them to get written about in newspapers) drinking Bell's whisky at a special tasting (helping them to get written about in newspapers) when a lady came up and said would he pose for a photograph for the whisky trade press. 'I haven't seen you since Chichester's funeral,' she said. 'Yes,' said Mr Hill, looking suitably solemn. 'What a fine man.' Mr Hill wasn't at the Chichester funeral but he saw no reason to be impolite, least of all to a firm which sponsors sport.

When he is not telling the great British public about football, this is the world Mr Hill moves in, helping sponsors across the road, being kind to distressed sports folk, introducing nice people to other nice people. It's a world he'll be moving around in even more from 1 January, when he'll no longer be London Weekend's Deputy Controller of Programmes.

He'll still be appearing as ever. He loves performing on the tele more than anything else – but he's giving up his TV executive jobs to run his own business as a sort of super sports consultant. It's not a world the general public know about but it's very lucrative. He'll probably end up a mlllionaire. But on the face of it, it seems a sad comedown for one of football's all-time originals.

Some cynics say he must know something we don't know. After all he got out of Coventry just before the decline. . . . 'That's not true. My motives are always the best. I know that's a lovely arrogant statement, but you need arrogance to be anybody. I gave lots of reasons at the time for leaving Coventry which were true but not the whole truth. I said I'd had five years as

50

a manager and that was enough for anyone. I said I wanted a rest. I said I wanted to do something different. Those were reasons why I was glad I'd made the decision. The real truth was that I didn't want to leave. I asked for a ten-year contract and they wouldn't give it to me.

'I'd had success from the beginning at Coventry, but I knew in the First Division it would take three or four years to settle down. I thought the board might become impatient. I knew the temperament of the chairman. It might all become sour if it took too long. I wanted a ten-year contract to make myself secure. When they refused I couldn't believe it. I thought they were my friends. I had to leave because I refused a five-year contract. I kept the differences secret at the time because I didn't want to embarrass the club. Now that they're doing well again it doesn't matter. But if they had given me the ten-year contract I have not the slightest doubt that Coventry would have won the First Division.'

It wasn't just in football terms that he was so successful at Coventry. The Sky Blue spirit he created survives to this day. In a world which is still basically feudal he was the first and, so far, the last reformer. He actively encouraged supporters to support rather than disown them which is what many clubs do. He organised the supporters' trains, laying on bingo and dancing in the guards' vans on the way there and on the way back his comments on the match were broadcast to all carriages. Their match programmes are still the best in the country.

'I set the pattern for football clubs ten years ago, but nobody has followed it. The object of most clubs seems to be to keep people out. There are few football directors with warmth or the intelligence to do what I did. Just little things, like having enough telephones with polite girls to welcome everyone who rings in. Have you ever tried to ring a football club? I made everybody welcome, from the lowest to the most important supporter. All clubs have their crypt-like inner sanctums which outsiders aren't allowed in. As a joke at Coventry I wanted a room which was so special nobody was allowed in.'

And look at how they treat the players. I made them into normal human beings in regard to pay and contract, but they still get treated like serfs during the week and executives on Saturday afternoon. How on earth can they do their best in those conditions? You've got to let their personalities blossom—then they'll be better players. If you could put the confidence I have as a person into the body of, say, Jimmy Pearce, what a player you'd have.

'I've given my advice for free for years and been ignored, perhaps now I'm setting up my own business people might act on it if they have to pay for it. I know at Coventry I was resented as a brash upstart. Clubs deliberately wouldn't copy me, even though I was offering a lifebelt. I'll now give advice to any club who comes to me, not about buying players but about the commercial running of a club. If Hayes United come to me, and promise to do exactly what I say, then I'd love to help.'

But in the main his new job will be getting sponsors to put money into sport. He says sport needs the money, so that must be good. 'You need an honest guy in the middle to see that both sides get good value. The Sportsman Club is my first client. I'm also doing a lot of charity work.

'It's nice to be on my own, just being Jimmy Hill. I enjoyed having titles. I loved being rung up as chairman of the PFA. I like to see my opinion being printed rather than letting someone else get away with something stupid. Positions matter because people are impressed by them, but I've had enough. I've done what I had to do as Head of Sport. I'd had enough of being Head of Publicity, seeing that everyone had a gin and tonic.'

But the new job itself, such as it is, sounds pretty valueless. Nothing, after all, can be more valueless than becoming a millionaire. When sport in the main is run by geriatrics, in mind if not in body, surely at 44 he still has something to contribute?

'Perhaps it is valueless. That's your opinion. I admit my happiest time was when I was playing for Fulham, even when at times the crowd didn't like me, and at the same time occupying my mind with the PFA. I'm always at my best when I've got a cause. But where are the causes? Nobody's come forward and asked me to do anything yet. I was asked to go to Coventry and asked to go to London Weekend. I could manage a club, but I did that ten years ago. If I could somehow manage all 92 clubs, that would be a challenge, breathing life into them. I'm fascinated by new things.

'I achieved things in football when I was young which is sad really, to think the pinnacle of my life might be behind me. If I died tomorrow, I'd be quite happy. I've had opportunities most people never dream about. Even being barracked at Fulham. In retrospect that was a pleasure, though I didn't think so at the time.'

This barracking which he's never forgotten, was partly to do with him being an awkward-looking player – made worse by playing alongside the incomparable Johnny Haynes. Now he's a polished performer in every sense, with the talents and energies to do almost anything he might set his mind to.

It's strange really that at London Weekend they didn't move him out of sport and really stretch him (perhaps that was what worried them). Now he's suffering the in-built problem of all whiz-kids: he's outstripped himself. He doesn't agree, maintaining that being a consultant will be a useful life. Why don't they make him secretary of the FA or the Football League or both? That would stretch him: and football.

1972

The Boss

BRIAN CLOUGH got into his silver Mercedes and drove himself home for lunch, still wearing the green nylon shirt and felt carpet slippers he'd been wearing all morning while he'd been watching his players training.

Football managers don't usually go in for leisurely lunches with their wives and families. Football managers usually eat football for lunch. As football managers go, Mr Clough is very strange. He has time for life other than football. As for the juxta-position of the flash car and the un-flash clothes, that's not really so strange, though his players think it's funny, even eccentric. Mr Clough is a mass of contradictions. In public, especially on TV, he's the man the country's football fans love to hate, the loud-mouth, the know-all. In private, well, the testimonies to his softness and kindness and humanity are almost embarrassing.

Back at Derby County FC's ground, home of the present champions of the Football League, a gaggle of local journalists were sitting in a room outside the shrine, patiently waiting for Cloughy to come back from his lunch and give them an audience.

'I cover about ten League clubs in the Midlands,' said one freelance journalist. 'Every Friday we call them and all we usually get is a list of 12 names. But with Cloughy, he always gives you a story. In the five years since he came to Derby, I can't tell you how much my salary's gone up every year. Just because of him. He's a genius.'

The hours went by. Mr Clough returned and padded in and out from time to time, supplying food and drink, saying a player wanted to see him, or his chairman was waiting, he wouldn't be long. Nobody was at all worried.

'I know I'll get some copy in the end,' said another journalist. 'He's murder to get on the phone and he's usually late for an appointment, but even London journalists, if they're prepared to come up and hang around, get something from him.'

Mr Clough's office is large and spacious with an enormous bar running across one side. He eventually had all the journalists lined up on one side, drinks in their willing hands, while he padded up and down, rampaging against his enemies, answering questions and shouting obscenities at a TV set which was blaring away in a corner. 'That's your opinion,' he kept on shouting when a TV sports expert on the box was giving his predictions.

One thing people with strong opinions can't stand is people with strong opinions.

'I don't regard winning the League as Utopia, though we still haven't had the credit we deserved for doing it. We did it with no gimmicks, unlike Leeds, and with the smallest pool of players in the Division. Whichever teams win the Championship in the next 20 years, and I hope teams like Rochdale and Halifax will be amongst them, none of them will have as hard a job as we had. We did it with 12 players. Those London bums can't explain it. All right, I admit we did it against the odds, but we did it with ability. Revie has been going crackers trying to explain it ever since. I give Allison and Shankly their due. They both said we could do it. But it's those bums on the Fleet Street sports pages I hate most. They called it a fluke. They wrote us off months before the season ended. They're so biased in favour of the London clubs it's revolting. Then when we did win, they weren't big enough or competent enough to get round it. They just ignored us. When I'm proved wrong, I'm big enough and competent enough to get round it. If I tell my lads they'll hammer Arsenal 2–0 and we don't, I'll think of some explanations, I'll find some reasons. I'll face up to it. But not those London bums. Right, last drinks. I've got my bairn's birthday party at four o'clock. You've got two more minutes.'

Brian Clough has had all sorts and conditions of bums to rail against, right throughout his life. He's always been the underdog, the one overlooked or under-rated, the one who's been told to shut up and don't be so aggressive, who do you think you are. There's no doubt he's thrived on it. This season, for the first time in his life, he's expected to do well. Naturally, his rivals have been gloating over some of his team's rather surprising defeats. Is he up to success?

In the car home he agreed that having people against him, having had things hard as a player, had been a spur, but at the same time he'd been made very unhappy. 'People talk about my career. What a bloody joke. I never had a career.'

He was born in Middlesbrough in 1936, one of six brothers and two sisters. His father used to work in a sweet factory. He went to the local secondary modern school, where he was no good academically and cared only about football, cricket and tennis. But he wasn't much good at them either; he never thought about being a footballer. At 15 he went into the offices of the local megalith – ICI – and worked for more than two years as a junior clerk in the Work Study department. Right from the first day he started lashing out at authority, though with little success.

'I was told that my clocking-in time would be 12 minutes past seven every morning. Twelve minutes past seven! Can you think of a bloody sillier time? I wanted to know which genius had thought up that, but they wouldn't tell me. How ICI has survived all these years by starting people at 12 minutes past seven I'll never know.'

He was playing park football at weekends, and when he was about 17,

Middlesbrough took him on as a part-timer, though with no promises of making him a professional. Soon after, he was called up for national service.

'That's when I came to my senses, from 18 to 20 in the Forces. I thought hell's teeth, what am I going to do with life? I'm not going back to ICI. So I wrote to Middlesbrough instead. I had to ask them to take me on as a professional. They didn't ask me.'

After six months in Middlesbrough's reserves, on £7 a week, he asked to go. 'I told them they were treating me unfairly. I said give us me cards, I'm going. They gave me a rise.' He got a few first-team games, then he dropped back into the reserves, feeling he was a failure.

'I was only the fourth choice for centre-forward. No one was telling me I could make it, so I was very depressed. At 21 you need your confidence boosted. At 25 you can strut around and look after yourself. The only person who convinced me I was any good was Peter Taylor, the first-team goalie. He was the first person to tell me I was bloody good. He said that in another set-up I could do really well. But the buggers wouldn't let me go. As a reserve they wouldn't transfer me, then when I made the first team they wouldn't let me go either. I don't know why.' When he finally made the first team, his success was phenomenal.

He was the prototype cannonball centre-forward, straight out of the boys' comics, who threw himself at every chance and scored goals like clockwork. He set up a goal-scoring record which still stands, 251 goals in 271 League matches. No footballer since the war has scored goals so quickly or so consistently or at such a young age as Brian Clough. (Dixie Dean in the Thirties is the only one who can match his record.) But by doing it all in Second Division matches he didn't get the national coverage and credit he was convinced he deserved. Eventually his goal-scoring ability did get him into the England team, but he got only two full caps in all. 'It was rank bad selection on the part of the England committee.'

Despite all his goals, he spent every season at Middlesbrough asking for a transfer, hoping to go to a First Division side, so he could really show them. Middlesbrough made him captain, hoping to keep him quiet, but this led to further trouble. A group of the players signed a round-robin, asking for him to be relieved of the captaincy. 'I don't know why they did it. All I know is there were a few scoundrels around at the time. I was very hurt. I took being captain very seriously.' He remained captain, but he was no happier. 'The only thing I enjoyed during my six years at Middlesbrough was scoring goals. From Saturday to Saturday I was very unhappy. My ability was never utilised, by me or the management. Only goals kept me sane. That was the only pleasure.'

At last, in 1961, he was transferred to Sunderland for £45,000. They were also in the Second Division, but two seasons later they were promoted to the First without Clough's help. On Boxing Day 1962, in a match against Bury, he injured his knee, an injury which finished his career. He was only 26. The injury dragged on for a further 18 months, as he tried to make a come-back –

he did return for three First Division games – but he eventually had to pack in playing. He helped on the coaching side for a bit at Sunderland and then was out of work for a while till Hartlepool took him on as manager in 1965, at the age of 29, making him the youngest manager in the country.

At Hartlepool he drove the team coach, went round the working men's clubs with cap in hand to get money to pay the players, and offered to go without his own salary to keep the club solvent. Nevertheless, he faced every issue head on, ducking no decisions. 'I didn't know up to then that I could be a manager, but I learned quickly. The biggest crime a player can commit is giving the ball away. The biggest crime for a manager is copping out of his word. I warned four players about their conduct. It didn't improve, so I said "Out", to all four of them. It left me with only seven players, but if a manager threatens something, he's got to keep his word.'

At Hartlepool he had as his assistant Peter Taylor, the same Peter Taylor who was his friend at Middlesbrough. Today, he's his assistant manager at Derby. Inside football it's known that Taylor has made an important contribution to Clough and to Derby, though the general public never hears about him. He's a perfect counterpoint, having no desire to hear himself talk or be talked about. But in many ways, despite the public image, Clough is not the hard man of Derby. It's Taylor who's the toughie.

In five years they've transformed Derby, taking them from the foot of the Second Division to the top of Divnsion One, doubling the gates, revitalising the club and the team. It's noticeable how many Derby directors have gone since Clough arrived, though the chairman, Sam Longson, who made the brave decision to bring him from Hartlepool, is still there and even carries a pin-up picture of Clough in his wallet.

There have been stories about Clough going to other, bigger and more glamorous clubs, or even taking over the England team, but he seems content at Derby. In November he signed a five-year contract. Despite a poor start in the League, Derby have managed to find enough form and spirit to beat Benfica in the European Cup. This means they're the last British team left in the competition (the next match will be in March) as Glasgow Celtic have been knocked out.

For a small club, they've reimbursed him well. Last season he made almost £20,000 with all the bonuses.

What a manager does to a team is abstract. You can't categorise it. It's a matter of inspiration. Most of his present stars came from lowly clubs, overlooked by other managers. He got McFarland, for example, now England's centre half, from Tranmere for £24,000. He also managed to coax that extra bit out of elderly stars like Dave Mackay, whom Spurs thought had had his day when they let him go for £4,000. Now, with success, he's in the money and can buy ready-made stars like £170,000 Colin Todd and £250,000 David Nish.

He has a passion for players of the right character, and he's willing to bawl out any shirkers in public, to humiliate them, to grind the skivers or phonies or cowards or cheats into the ground, whether it is players or journalists. (He has his acolytes now, but over the years quite a few journalists have been told they weren't wanted at his club.)

'I haven't found a compensation yet for scoring goals. I fed on goals. They were ecstasy to me. It was like a bloody drug. But scoring the quickest 250 goals in history wasn't enough. I never got to Wembley. I never won a Championship. I would love to have been one of Derby's 12 who did it last year. Playing is the biggest pleasure.'

There were shouts of delight as he arrived home in his Mercedes. He was slightly late for the party, but they were all waiting for him, 16 eight-year-old boys. The party was for Simon, his eldest. He has another son, Nigel, six, and a daughter Elizabeth, who is five. He went in, clapped his hands and told them to get ready. He has had 14 kids in his Mercedes, but he decided 16 was too many, so they all set off down the suburban street, running behind him, shouting: 'We are the Champions.' We got to a park and he arranged two sides and started them playing. He was to be the referee, though Elizabeth was to stay beside him and do the actual whistle-blowing.

An onlooker could easily have thought he was slightly deranged. He wasn't running a children's party game between two sets of eight-year-olds. It was deadly serious. He treated the kids as real professional footballers, which of course they responded to. He padded up and down in his carpet slippers, screaming out instructions, like that schoolmaster in the football match in *Kes* who was convinced he was running Manchester United.

'Do that once more, Si, and you're off!' he shouted at his eight-year-old son. 'Who said you could pick that ball up ? The whistle didn't blow for a throw-in, did it? No, it did not. Handball!'

He let them get away with nothing, not even foul throw-ins, though their little arms weren't really up to it. He made them line up while he demon-strated the correct way.

Even his five-year-old daughter, Elizabeth, who was supposed to blow every time he told her, didn't escape his wrath. 'I've warned you, Lib. If you bugger around any more I'll take the whistle.'

His wife Barbara was duly grateful when they all trailed back to the house for the birthday tea, all nicely quietened and exhausted. He watched them getting stuck into the goodies then went into his front room and opened a bottle of champagne.

'What do you mean, I'm now coming on all middle class ? You can say I live in a middle-class house. You can say I've got a middle-class car. Say what you bloody like. It's only your opinion. This house isn't middle class. It's bloody Buckingham Palace.

'I'm still a Socialist and always will be, but that doesn't stop me having the best car. I can get our three kids in it, plus the wife and me Mam and Dad, all in comfort, that's why I have it. The club car when I came here was a Vauxhall Victor, but I didn't want that. I asked them to buy me a Mercedes last year but they wouldn't. So I said stuff it, I'll buy one myself.'

He says his Socialism is from the heart, not his head, and always has been. Over the years he's been asked several times to stand as a Labour MP and has seriously considered it. He has a charity box for leukaemia research on the bar in his office. He's talked all his staff into giving up part of their salaries to Oxfam. During the miners' strike he gave out free tickets for Derby matches to the pickets.

'I just have to read the papers to know I'm a Socialist. Look at all the millions not being fed. Look at the political prisoners. Look at the discrimination everywhere, not just colour but class, education and privilege of all sorts. I'm lucky. I've got three well fed, superbly looked after kids. When I saw the pictures of those dead kids in Biafra I burst into tears.

'People in football are surprised I'm a Socialist. Their apathy generally is staggering, which I think is an indictment of my profession. They say sport and politics don't mix, which is rubbish. It's like saying you don't need oxygen to breathe. You can't have one without the other on this earth. I think people who want to keep politics out of sport are a bit simple.'

In practice as a manager he tries to follow his principles, such as never discriminating, except against the louts and skivers. There's one London team which has him frothing at the mouth, just because he maintains a spiv element has been allowed to take over. 'If you threaten certain spiv players, you must carry it out and not let them get away with it. A football team has only 11 players. It just needs one bad 'un to affect the rest. In ICI, with thousands and thousands of people, you can afford to carry some scoundrels. Not in a football team.'

He's fanatical about education, insisting that each apprentice who joins the club at 15 goes to the local Polytechnic for one full day and two evenings each week till he's a full professional. Most managers allow young players time off for study, but not many make it compulsory. 'I can't guarantee to turn boys into professional footballers at Derby, but they'll end up well educated. I've got one boy, 16-year-old Steve Powell, who's doing three A-levels. I've got another doing a degree. In this democracy in which we live, education is available to all despite the public schools trying to make it exclusive. Give me any time a talented football player who's also intelligent. Show me a talented player who's thick, and I'll show you a player with problems.'

If his heart is therefore in the right place, if he's kind to children, contributes generously to charity and always helps dumb footballers across the road, why then do so many people dislike him?

It's all to do with his TV appearances. One minute he says he loves it, admitting he laps it up and yes, he must be vain, and the next he's trying to pretend he does it as a duty, because it's an honour for Derby. 'There are 92 football managers, give or take the six or seven who are about to be sacked every season, so I think it's a compliment to Derby that the BBC should choose me for their football panels.'

There's no doubt he loves it, despite all the abuse he's had to take over the years. 'I have had some terrible stick. I know many viewers say bloody hell, not that bugger again. But there's now been a complete switch. I'm not bulling you, because I never bull, but I promise you letters have suddenly changed. They now say I'm right.

'The thing is, people never listen to what you say on the telly. All they notice is your manner. I can't help my voice. I can't help my manner. I can't help how I look. If people disagreed with what I say, that would be one thing, but it's how I say it that gets them.'

Internationally, his manner has led to a few rows in the BBC. He's not very good, for example, at controlling his bad language. He called Sir Alf Ramsey 'a stubborn bugger'. During the World Cup they put him with a panel of nine, which he thought was ridiculous. 'It was a silly set-up so I just messed round. They then saw sense and agreed with me.

'I'm against any rehearsing and always refuse to do it. I've also refused to have Bob Wilson talking about managerial problems, not when I'm on any-way. He's a player and he knows nothing about management. I won't have it.'

Now and again, when he sees himself as others see him, he's a bit appalled. 'I came home once and watched a recording of a sports pro-gramme I'd been on and I thought, bloody hell, that's not me, is it? What a big-headed, dogmatic bastard. So next time I tried to calm down. It meant they got themselves a crappy interview.

'I only get upset if the wife's upset. She did once say I'd been extremely rude to someone. Sometimes I do set out to be rude, but that time I hadn't meant it. I hate me Mam getting upset, that's even worse.

'I suppose I've got more intelligent and wiser over the years, but I'm not going to try and change myself now. It doesn't bother me what people think.

'They say I've got chips on my shoulder, but I don't think so. I just believe in giving my opinion. I don't say it's the right opinion. I just say it's mine. They tell me that in giving my opinions I shout, that I say things other people wouldn't say, but bloody hell, you've got to shout, when kids in Vietnam are having bombs dropped on them. OK, I have got a chip on my shoulder, if it means shouting out about what's wrong with the world. And OK I'm stupid and ignorant enough to think my opinions are right. Have some more champagne. To absent friends, those buggers in London. You wouldn't believe the pleasure I've had out of drinking their health.'

At 36, he's the youngest manager to win the First Division. Apart from walking on the water, or being Prime Minister, what else is there to do ?

'I wouldn't mind being Prime Minister. I wouldn't take the yacht, but I'd have a go at it, if I thought I could do it. So far all I've found I can do is be a football manager. I can't see myself doing this for ever. I can't visualise myself at the age of 55 still in this game. At times I do think I'll give it up. Times like when we get beat at home. Times when I've got to go out and spend £200,000 on a player. Times when I have to go into the dressing-room and shout at them, knowing that one of these days some player is going to say balls to you, and walk out on me.

'I have thought about getting out of football altogether, now that I've won something. But I've only been a manager seven years. I'm only on the threshold of my career. I've got a lifetime to go. I got cheated as a player. I don't want to be cheated as a manager.'

JOHNSTON.

BUIST. MEADE. RUSSELL. BOYLAM. BOYLE. CRAWFORD. POWELL. DAVIS.
SINCLAIR. DUFF. BROCK. Mc. AVOY. CARVER.

Photo by Tasma.

· Woolwich

HAYWOOD. BOYD. O'BRIEN. FAIRCLOUGH.
WOOLWICH ARSENAL.

1973

Clough Collapse

Brighton 2 Bristol Rovers 8

IT WAS a bad case of bravado that brought Brian Clough to Brighton as their new manager. Yesterday, in the most amazing, hilarious, crazy, splendid and constantly enjoyable match of the season, bravado turned to masochism.

Mr Clough should have retired from football at the top, as he always said he would, and done something worthwhile with his life, like playing with his kids or running Shelter, or even poncing around on the tele. Look at those First Division managers still apparently at the top – Ramsey, Shankly, Revie and Nicholson. There they all are, continually trying to repeat the old success. Very sad. The only lesson to be learned from success is that it's a load of nothing. Having done it once, you've got to move on.

Mr Clough is now at the bottom, or even below, after yesterday. If he had to stay in football his place is at the top. He could have dictated British football from Derby, putting directors in their place, if there is a place in football for directors, and turning footballers into all-round human beings who enjoy doing their job, neither of which is the case at the moment.

It will prove nothing about Clough if he drags Brighton up by their jockstraps. He's done all that before. This time, alas, it looks highly unlikely. Bristol trampled them into the ground and apart from one player there was not a hopeful sign in the Brighton team.

Rovers are a solid workmanlike team with two terrific old-fashioned goal scorers, Warboys and Bannister, who between them got seven terrific old-fashioned goals. In Bristol they're now known as Smash and Grab.

They're both from Yorkshire, both been around with other clubs, and yesterday they both had their photographs in the Football League handout, just to let the whole of English football have a good look at them.

Warboys is the smasher. He's big and strong, a real heavy with long sideboards, and a lolloping stride. He looked clumsy at first and when he ran round Gall, Brighton's centre-half, in the fourth minute, he made it look so easy that one could hardly believe it. From his cross the pattern of the match was set when Bannister grabbed the first goal.

As the game went on, Warboys started to take his time and shed his clumsiness and showed what a controlled and powerful player he is.

He took a through ball from Bannister for his second, rounded the goalie and scored. The next one was even more difficult; the ball was bobbling and three Brighton men were trying to hang on to him. He managed to control the ball, keep them off, look up and shoot – all on the run.

Bannister, the Grabber, is short and stocky with curling long hair, baggy shorts and very cocky. He got his hat-trick in the first half. After only a minute of the second half he was standing in the Brighton goalmouth waiting for a corner kick. The Rovers fans were screaming his name and he ran and gave them a cheer in return. Acknowledging applause with 44 minutes to go. The cheek.

As for Brighton, on yesterday's showing they have only one player with any skill and that's O'Sullivan but he's somehow not strong enough to forage on his own. The defence was abysmal. There was a feeling of Bristol constantly having four forwards to each Brighton defender. Spearritt and Ley tried hard to calm things down but with no success.

The crowd loved it all, even the Brighton supporters, though they grew a trifle sarcastic towards the end.

When Howell got Brighton's second rather pathetic goal, making it 8–2 against them, the home crowd shouted 'Easy, easy.'

In the press box, everyone was in a sweat, trying to keep up with the goals. The bloke beside me from the *Mirror* arrived half an hour late – missing the first six goals.

Mr Clough gave us his all after the match, which was very funny and will no doubt be over every sports page today and on tele this afternoon. The Bristol manager wasn't at all funny. 'I was disappointed. We gave away two goals for the first time this season.'

Mr Clough certainly brings drama with him. There is doubtless more to come.

Ground: firm. Weather: bright.

Goals: Bannister (4 min), 0–1; Fearnley (11 min), 0–2; O'Sullivan (20 min), 1–2; Bannister (29 min) 1–3; Bannister (31 min), 1–4; Warboys (37 min), 1–5; Warboys (46 min), 1–6; Warboys (55 min), 1–7; Warboys (65 min), 1–8; Howell, 2–8.

Brighton (4–3–3): Powney; Templeman, Ley, Spearritt, Gall; Howell, Towner, Beamish; Hilton, Robertson, O'Sullivan.

Bristol Rovers (4–3–3); Eadie; Jacobs, Parsons, Green, Taylor; Prince, Fearnley, Stanton; Warboys, Bannister, Dobson.

Referee: T. W. Dawes (Suffolk).

1973

He'll Do it His Way . . .

THE LOOK on Steve Heighway's face after the 1971 FA Cup Final was something you rarely see in football. Liverpool had been beaten by Arsenal, and it was the end of their world, their life, their purpose. The dressing-room contained the hulks of shipwrecked souls. Smith and Toshack had become dehumanised. It was best to avert your eyes. Yet there was Heighway smiling an eager, boyish, excited, glowing smile.

In 1971, Steve Heighway was something that rarely happens in football. He'd arrived as a complete outsider, straight from university, brought up in a middle-class home, untrained and uncoached, a free and natural spirit, not a battery farm footballer who'd been force-fed from the age of 13. He might just as well have landed from Mars.

It wasn't, therefore, surprising that he was excited at Wembley that day. He would have liked to have won, but as a normal human being, the pleasures of the occasion had not been wasted on him.

He's now had three full seasons as a Liverpool star. Has he ceased to be a normal human being, and become a footballer?

'It all happened so suddenly that first year. I didn't know what was going on. Until that year I'd never had the slightest intention of becoming a professional footballer. All I wanted to be was a teacher.'

He'd just graduated from the University of Warwick, getting a second in politics and economics, and was about to do a teachers' course. One day he got a phone call at his digs in Coventry to say that some Liverpool scouts had seen him playing for British Universities, and that the manager was coming to see him in person.

'I was completely unimpressed. It was nothing to do with my life. Mr Shankly came and went on about all the money I'd get as a first-team player. I said, "Oh yes, but your reserve players, how much do they get?" He wouldn't talk about me being in the reserves.

'I was about to get married, and my wife was even less impressed than I was. But we decided that even on a reserve player's salary we could buy a house – something we'd never manage for years on a teacher's pay. It might be interesting for a couple of years to do something else. I'm not a confident person. I didn't expect to succeed. I never do. I took it for the money.

'Looking back, I was very naïve that first year. I just went my merry way. If

I had a bad game, I thought, "Too bad." I carried on as I'd always done, messing around, not facing problems seriously, being a bit of a clown.

'I realise now that the team didn't like me that first year. I probably knew it at the time, but never worried about it. I was probably rather aloof.'

The fruits of his three years of success are easy to see. He has a large detached £20,000 house beside the sea at Ainsdale, near Southport. He and his wife, who's a primary school teacher, both have cars. His income is ten times what he'd be getting as a teacher.

But he's by no means flash. They have a two-year-old son, Jamie, and all three take a simple camping holiday each year. He saves rather than spends, and thinks footballers are not paid enough compared with other entertainers.

That's the first sign that the process of footballisation has had an effect on Mr Heighway. There are others. Like almost all footballers, he hates the football Press.

'In the football system they are the weak link. They've never played football, and they know nothing about it. That first year they were saying nice things, even though I knew they were getting it all wrong. When they said nasty things, I was very hurt, even though I knew they were still getting it all wrong.

'I decided that as neither the good nor the bad was true, I should give them up. For almost three years, I've never read the back pages. I think the standard of popular sports reporting is disgustingly low. The serious papers get it all wrong by over-complicating what is a simple game. I have no confidence in any soccer reporter to write about soccer.

'I never watch our matches on TV either. I know how I've played on Saturday. I know my mistakes. I want to get away from it. TV can't make you a better player.

'The reaction to our defeat by Red Star was typical of the fickleness of the Press and public. No one could call them a great side. All we didn't do was take our chances. I think the criticism of England's defeat by Poland was equally unfair.

'A soccer reporter should not try to entertain or amuse, but to inform. But they can't. They don't understand what it is like to play soccer.'

Heighway now knows what it's like to be in the public eye, in good times and in bad, which is why he has such sympathy for all players. And like all players, he's also found that what happens inside a club can be the hardest of all.

'It's the huge emotional ups and downs. I can't take it. There's an enormous high created when you win, but three days after I feel washed out. I begin to doubt my capabilities. The happy moments don't last long. Then, when we lose, I feel consumed with guilt and worries. It's not a natural thing, being a professional footballer.

'At the same time, there's the physical strain. It drains you completely. You should see the lads on Monday, especially towards the end of the season. Their backs are aching, they can hardly stand up.

'I sit on the coach after a match and think, I'm packing it up. I wasn't fitted for this game.'

Naturally enough, he now feels part of the team. They're relaxed with him, having been through so much together. He still doesn't play cards, except when requested to make up a hand, but he knows exactly why they play. They find the boredom of travelling unbearable. He still prefers to chat or read.

Rather surprisingly, he's not particularly close to Brian Hall, Liverpool's other graduate, though they're friends. His three closest friends in the team are Keegan, Cormack and Boersma. He's now one of them, for better or for worse.

His wife thinks it is for the worse. She says he's changed in the three years, become harder, less sensitive. He thinks he probably has changed. He certainly worries more. Even though he's now an insider, he can see only too clearly what the system does to its players. The normal player accepts it, having known nothing else.

'A manager is paid to get the team on the field, and secure the best result. That's his job. But there must be other ways of getting good results. I don't really want to go into the manipulation of people, but that's what it is.

'In other forms of management, there is an attempt to handle each person in a different way. Football managers are untrained as managers, and they know only one method, total dedication, because that's what they have. In a way, the worst sort of footballers become managers. Only the fanatical would be silly enough to do it. They have to have the drive of Hitler. Our guy never lets you relax. The constant need is to win trophies. He never lets up.

'The right way to manage footballers might be completely the opposite way – to encourage them to relax. People need to be educated to relax. I'm like the rest of them now. I can't relax. It must be wrong. I've seen my doctor and he's suggested tranquillisers. I've refused them. I feel that would really be the end. But I need something.

'Managers don't worry that players can be totally destroyed by the time they're 30. They don't care when you're ill, if you're on the treatment table, or when you're in the reserves. You have to be a strong man to be a footballer. No wonder the weak go to the wall. Thank God it's a short life.'

What makes it worse for Heighway, compared with the normal player, is that he has an alternative. When other footballers feel fed up, they have a simple rationalisation – but for football, so they keep saying, they'd be nobodies. Every footballer is child-like in his gratitude to the game.

'I'm always arguing with them about this. I tell them they owe football nothing.' His feelings have been heightened this season because the team hasn't had such a great start, not by Liverpool's standards, but now they're hitting their best again.

'I sensed the crowd turning against us at Anfield, yet in over three seasons I've never lost at Anfield in a League match. The standards are so very high that you get the team sitting in the bath depressed after a 1–0 win.'

Like most players, he enjoyed his schoolboy football more than the professional game. 'As a player, I must be better equipped today. I am now an effective player, if your conception of an effective player is Liverpool's conception of an effective player. I don't feel overtrained, a stereotyped footballer. The manager does encourage us to express our individuality.

'I'm still learning because I'm a perfectionist. I want to win. The trouble is, I now think about it constantly, worry about it far too much.'

He thinks that all footballers should be paid enough so that at 27, if they want to, they can retire from football, before the real humiliations begin. Heighway is 26 tomorrow. All afternoon, he'd talk as if his own retirement was imminent. Why doesn't he?

'I do look on this as a transitional stage. The best in my life is yet to come. That's what keeps me going. But at this moment I feel part of the team, loyal to the lads. I don't want to appear just a flash in the pan. And the highs, they're still as great as ever.

'When I cross-examine myself on all my motives – and I do so all the time – I think the main one is materialistic. It's the weakness of mankind. I now need the high wage to pay my high mortgage. I don't want to become a teacher and have to struggle. I want to be a *good* teacher with no worries.

'I'm keener than ever to get into teaching. The longer I stay a footballer I realise that I'll miss the lads and the competition, but the day I pack it in I'll have an almighty sense of relief.'

1974

Paine Barrier

THERE SEEMS to have been a spate of football anniversaries this season, enough to bring tears to the eye. Is it because players are playing longer, or are the fans becoming sentimentally soft in the head? Last week, at Leeds, George Armstrong was presented with a set of candelabras and some champagne after playing something like two million matches for Arsenal.

Last week Terry Paine celebrated his three million years with Southampton. Alas, yesterday's match was cancelled, but he will still be presented with a silver salver by his chairman. That's nice.

To be exact, and suitably serious, Mr Paine is celebrating 800 League and Cup games for Southampton. He's the longest serving one-club player in the game – at least, he hasn't come across anyone else who's done 18 consecutive seasons with the same club. In many ways, he is a rare specimen – one of the few England wingers still in captivity. Anthropologically, his sideburns are worth a study themselves. Didn't we all cut them off when we stopped being Teddy Boys? Mr Paine didn't. It meant that when they came back into fashion, he was already there.

His first game was in 1957 at the age of 17. He's gone with Southampton from the Third Division to the First, which is one of the reasons he's never left them. On the rare occasions he's been fed up, the team moved forward.

Perhaps his most amazing achievement, apart from simply surviving, is that in all those 18 seasons he has not missed more than nine games through injury. The recent clampdown on full frontal brutality has obviously given him a new lease of life, but even before then he'd been miraculously free of injuries. 'I'm a good jumper,' he explains.

As a lad, coaches used to worry when he couldn't touch his toes. He didn't; he's not a worrier. Then it was found that he has incredibly short hamstrings. 'It still baffles the coaches, and I still can't touch my toes. But they've never given me a second's trouble in all my playing life.'

He was dropped a few times a couple of years ago under the previous manager, when it was thought he was too old for two games a week. 'If a team is doing badly, it's the old fellows who get dropped first. I soon showed them, though. I pride myself on being very fit. It's easier now, if anything, because I think this present Southampton team is the best I've played in.'

Like most oldsters, Terry Paine thinks the enjoyment is now less for the spectator than it was, what with the tactics and the defensive play. There is less enjoyment for the players as well – 'though defensive play has helped to keep many bad players in the First Division; good teamwork can counter their faults'. But he feels that attacking, flowing football is on the way back, thanks to the breed of new young managers, especially his own. 'Look around the First Division – where you've got a young manager you've got an attractive team, Bloomfield, Milne, Jago and our Laurie McMenemy. They're the best hope for English football today.'

He's got his business enterprises lined up – a fruit and veg shop, a café, and a block of flats. He was a Southampton councillor for three years, and intends to go back to politics one day. (His prophecy: 'The General Election will be very, very close.') All the same, despite being 35 next month, he sees his future in football stretching ahead for several seasons.

If Southampton are to keep putting on the style, they will play Terry Paine as long as possible. They're the lucky ones. Last night's *Match of the Day* would have been lucky as well, if Southampton's match had been televised as planned. Mr Paine had trimmed his sideboards specially.

G. CRAWLEY.   J. HODGKINSON.
W. DAWSON.   S. MESTON.   W. MC. MILLAR.   H. HAYNES   D. MC. KAY.   H. ISAAC

Photo by R. Hider.   Sheerness.

W. NAUGHTON.   J. FARRELL.   J. TURNER.
R. BUCHANAN.   W. KEAY.

SOUTHAMPTON St. MARY'S.

1974

Weak at the Knees

I PLAYED football last Sunday. OK, don't say it, I know I shouldn't have done, not at my age and in my condition, when will you grow up and stop trying to be so flash and see some sense and no one thinks any the better of you, you know, not that I care, of course, it's your own decision and if you want to be stupid, go right ahead.

She doesn't, of course, say any of those things. Not any more. She just nods her head, says fine, and looks away, preoccupied by something much more important, such as cleaning the green mould off the new lemons, bought only last Tuesday at Sainsbury's, in those yellow plastic wire bags, and now look at them, what a disgrace.

But her posture speaks paragraphs and the way she says, 'Fine,' could fill pages. It's a clever game, oh you can't tell me anything about tame psychology. She knows that by saying *don't* I'll just go ahead and do it, so she says nuffink.

It had to be done, I said, several times. I *had* to play football last Sunday. No response. She was now giving the rest of the lemons a quick rub, before putting them back in their yellow cages.

She knows fine well why I had to play football last Sunday. I've been through that rationale several times, with maps and drawings, before and after, quotations get extra marks. The reason was very simple. I have bought a new pair of football boots.

At the age of 43 can you think of any more marvellous affirmation in the future, any more positive gesture I could make to show that I believe the best is yet to come and that this wonderful life is still worth living and that, God willing, I intend to be part of it for many years yet? Hmm? There you are, then. Not a pair of boots but a symbolic gesture.

Some blokes go off to Switzerland and spend a fortune on monkey glands. All I did was go down Kentish High Road to this nasty sport and camping shop I don't usually frequent, as there's an even cheaper – sorry nicer – sports shop much nearer, but it was closed, and there I lashed out and bought a pair of brand new Puma football boots, price £13.99. Yes, I could have bought the best Adidas and spent up to £40, but that would have been going it a bit. After all, I am 43 and five months. Let's not be *too* positive about the future.

I came home glowing, rejuvenated, a song in my heart and a jaunt in my gait and just a slight mote in my eye, half wondering if that pair at £12.99, despite being a size too small, might have done me just as well. Ah, that lovely smell of new-mown plastic and the rustle of virgin white tissue paper as I unwrapped the box when I reached home. Look what Daddy's got here, folks, come and see what Hunt has gone and been and done. They all rushed the other way.

I wore them for supper, but still they wouldn't make the slightest comment. So before pudding I went upstairs and quickly put on my shorts and Dartmouth Park United shirt as well. The rotten lot. Not even a snigger. Jealous, all of them. Just wait till they are 43. They think I live in a fantasy world, but we'll see how many of them are perfect physical specimens at the age of 43.

I have played for Dartmouth Park United for about ten years now, man and superman, our Sunday morning Hampstead Heath team.

I wanted to hang on till I was 40, that was the first little Everest I was aiming at. Then I set my sights on hanging on till Jake became a fully fledged member. He is now 14 and a mid-field maestro, strong in the tackle, quick on the swearing, very hard on the old. I think he's a bit embarrassed by me now. He was such a podgy little fellow when he started, slow and hesitant, obviously in awe of my marvellous ball control and speed and stamina. Now the bread rolls have been reversed. I'm the podgy little fellow, as he's always telling me. I say so what, look at Puskas, he was podgy even at his height. I didn't know cats played football, said Jake. Ho ho, very funny.

Since Christmas, I haven't played *every* Sunday, not like the old days when I never missed. I have put the family first, now and again, and taken Flora to clarinet or the family on an outing. And sometimes I have not felt quite one hundred per cent.

Oh, the lads have still called for me. Is Hunt coming out to play, Mrs Davies. Some of these lads are 47, and one is even 50, but they'll always be lads to me, hey ho. It happens to be my ball, so they *have* to call for me. I also hold all the GLC pitch permits. I'm not daft. How do you think I get a game?

I put my boots on last Sunday morning and I was there, ready and waiting, when the chaps turned up. I had tried to scuff them up a bit, kick a few tables, take the worst off the shine, as I didn't want any smart remarks. Like stupid sixth formers, some of these 50-year-old grandfathers.

I was terrific for the first half hour, zooming up and down in my new boots, like Peter Pan, springing into every attack, haring back to defend, or do I mean Pegasus with the winged thingies. Then I decided to take a quick pot shot at goal, from quite a long way out, but I was convinced the old magic had come back. In doing so, I stubbed my toe. That was it. The Hagony Ivy was Hellish. I struggled on down the wing till the end, somehow, some way, they'll never say I'm a quitter, then I came home and went to bed early with hot-water bottles.

It is now Thursday and as I sit here typing this I am getting some very strange looks from the workmen on the roof next door. They obviously think we're running a kinky massage parlour, a new Streatham party house for middle-aged gents.

I am in my underpants. I have tried it with my trousers on, but I fear I might electrocute myself. Then those leering workmen would really have a larf.

Around my right thigh I have strapped a Three Heat Electric Pad which I

Dartmouth Park United FC, c. 1980: Hampstead Heath's finest set of Sunday-morning strollers. H. Davies is in the front row, fourth from the left. Also note Bernard Donoughue (now Lord Donoughue) standing, second from left, and Melvyn Bragg, still Melvyn Bragg, standing, fourth from the right

bought at Boots this morning, price £10.50. I'm keeping the bill in case I can persuade the taxman it was a literary injury. It's a sort of small electric blanket, about two feet long, which you wrap around the sore bit and then switch on, to one of three heats, and bingo, it's like being in the electric chair.

The instructions are frightening. You are warned in bold type not to jerk, insert pins into the pad, use in contact with modacrylic fibres, use in bed, keep on for excessive periods of time and certainly *Do Not Use Unattended.* How could I do that? Saw my leg off and walk away?

One of the main problems is that I can't actually do anything or go anywhere. It's taken me half an hour to connect it to the same switch as my electric typewriter, using a double plug, which is probably also something you should never do. I thought how clever, to sit and type and get better at the same time, but if I move one inch or breathe too quickly, either the

71

typewriter or the electric blanket cuts off. Should I completely forget and cross my legs, I'll probably fry instantly.

Then on my left leg, you are concentrating, I have strapped to my other knee a special hot water pad. It's like one of those freezing packs you take on picnics to keep things cold, only this is one you heat up in a pan of boiling water. A very kind Indian assistant at Boots persuaded me this would also be very efficacious. Quite cheap, as well, only £3.34.

Perhaps I should have got two water pads and saved on the electric torture instrument. The pad keeps slipping and slithering, that's the worst thing, even though I have tied it on with an old bandage. I'm trying not to touch it for another five minutes, if I live that long.

I've just realised my door is open. I can't move now, can I, not when all systems are go and the heat is at boiling point, but I know what will happen. Twice already this morning my wife has shown people straight up to my room, the rotten lot, knowing I'm sitting here like this. One of them was a young wife, new in the area, whom I've been trying to impress.

In front of me is a tube of Boots Pain Relieving Balm, just a small 35-gram tube, only 52p.

I know I have got only two legs and they are covered with sufficient equipment already, but to we athletes, a little tube of glycol monosalicylate will always come in handy. When all this unpleasantness is over, a new unpleasantness will doubtless come along.

They say Time is the Great Healer but really Heat is the Greatest Healer. Perhaps I should tie a hot bag to my head from now on. At 43, I really should be cured by now of all childish notions.

1974

Carlisle Hit the First Division

IT'S 71 years since Carlisle United was formed and most of that time they have been Nowhere. Now suddenly they have arrived from Nowhere – into the First Division. There is hope for us all.

Alan Ashman brought his whole playing staff, all 19 of them, down from Carlisle to witness this very wonderful occasion and said: 'Breathe it in, lads, it's a historic moment.' As a footballing occasion it was all truly wonderful for we long-standing Carlisle supporters.

They amazed Chelsea, and no doubt themselves, with a goal in the first minute. Balderstone floated in a free kick which man-mountain Droy missed, Houseman watched, and Green, Carlisle's gangling captain, trundled in at the second attempt.

Their second goal came ten minutes before half-time when O'Neill cheekily lobbed over Bonetti. In between, it has to be admitted through gritted teeth, Chelsea put on most of the pressure, especially in the first half, and had some very near misses. Having said that, very quickly, Carlisle could have scored twice in the last ten minutes when they turned on some exhibition stuff.

Carlisle crept into the First Division practically unnoticed – except by those clever clogs who yesterday morning were tipping them as the team most likely to go down 'Nobody tipped us to come up last season,' said Mr Ashman afterwards. 'I see that all the big fish we left behind are again being tipped to come up. Everybody could be wrong once more.'

They have no stars, no reserves, no loot, no crowd (an average of 8,000 is a huddle, not a crowd) and, until yesterday, none of the Chelsea swanks would have recognised any Carlisle player if he'd met him in his porridge (an old Border saying). What Carlisle have is a team style. It is to be hoped the television people give them some space to be seen – though BBC's *Grandstand* started badly yesterday lunchtime by naming Frank Clarke as Carlisle's star to watch and putting up a photograph of Frank Clark of Newcastle United.

Carlisle confounded Chelsea by building up from the back, never panicking, and never belting it – a collective calmness exemplified by Chris Balderstone, the man of the match. He played in the back four last season, but yesterday moved up to midfield, making way for new signing Parker from Coventry.

John Gorman, Carlisle's nearest thing to a star, did many star things, such as galloping overlaps and interchanging with Balderstone, which were a joy to watch. Hughie McIlmoyle, back with Carlisle for the third time, linked well with Frank Clarke – who went off injured in the second half – but tired towards the end.

Carlisle's attack can be a bit thin at times and with injuries it could be in real trouble by the end of the season. But their midfield and their back four youngsters are going to swallow some bigger and better fish than Chelsea could produce yesterday.

Chelsea have got £200,000 players and a brave new neo-brutal £2m stand, while Carlisle have got sheep and the excitement of £250 from this season's sponsored matches. Carlisle made Hay, while their sun was shining, look a very moderate player and in the second half he disappeared. Houseman has been brought back so far, from winger to full-back, that next week he'll probably be goalie.

Chelsea these days play a physical game, bulldozing into the box and banging away, which is typical of so many English teams I don't want to watch. Carlisle with far fewer individual skills, played to their talent as a unit and produced pure football. They have arrived triumphantly in the First Division, having crept quietly all the way from the Fourth. If they can do it there is hope for everyone.

Carlisle is good for football. Some good football, as we shall see this season, will come from Carlisle. End of commercial.

Weather: sunny. Pitch: firm.

Goals: Green (1 min), 0–1; O'Neill (76 min), 0–2. Chelsea (4–3–3): Bonetti; Locke; Houseman, Hollins, Droy; Harris, Kember, Hay; Garland (sub. Cooke, 75 min), Garner, Sissons.

Carlisle United (4–3–3): Ross; Carr, Gorman, O'Neill, Green; Parker, Train, Balderstone; McIlmoyle, Clark (sub, Martin 65 min), Laidlaw.

1974

Carlisle United 1 Tottenham 0

THEY SAID Chelsea were a load of dummies. They said Middlesbrough were jumped-up heavies. Now they'll have to say that Spurs are hasbeens. Anything to dismiss Carlisle, putting them down as a lucky team. Yesterday Spurs were the lucky team. Carlisle played 90 minutes of total flowing optimistic, happy, creative football and absolutely trounced the Tottenham team.

If luck, as opposed to consummate skill, had been on Carlisle's side they would have won 3–0. The referee at one stage gave a second penalty – Carlisle having scored from the spot in the 20th minute – but a linesman said it was inches out. Then Ray Train hit the underside of the bar and somehow the ball bounced out.

There has been an air of excitement in the town all week. Being top of the First Division if only for 24 hours, doesn't happen every year. A local meat firm got carried away to the extent of offering Carlisle's best player of the year a pound of Cumberland sausages, delivered to the door, every Friday.

Such promises would go to anyone's head. And yesterday morning the stars of the national press started arriving, having looked up Carlisle on their maps. Why, even Danny Blanchflower came. I hope he had the grace to look the other way on the rare occasion that Spurs got the ball.

From the kick-off Spurs looked a dejected team. Goalless and pointless, they were obviously worried by Carlisle's new found reputation and treated them from the beginning as overdogs. They lined up defensively, with Pratt being brought back into the side instead of McGrath and England for Keith Osgood. ('The time has come to give the youngsters a go,' said Spurs only last week. Two defeats. Out they went.) Perryman's first kick of the ball was a panic pass to Pratt, who was lying prone on the ground at the time, but in the fourth minute Perryman did fly back to tackle Balderstone, who was all on his own with only Jennings to beat. Laidlaw, who had a brilliant game, was beating England at will and the whole Spurs defence was soon falling over backwards in retreat every time he got the ball. It was England who gave away the penalty. He stuck out what looked like a wooden leg which he had sneaked on to the pitch without the referee noticing, and down came Laidlaw, who once again was steaming through. Jennings saved Balderstone's first attempt but the referee made him take it again – it looked as if Jennings might have moved—but Balderstone's second attempt, this time right into the right-hand corner, was hard and true. Train's near miss a minute later was a brilliant piece of opportunism, floating over a ball on the rebound with Jennings miles out of his goal.

The first stage of Spurs' demoralisation took the form of petty fouls and arguments with team-mates. The next stage, which lasted for the rest of the match, consisted of standing still after hitting the ball and either looking appealing or appalled. In the first half only Neighbour in the Spurs side looked as if he had played football before.

In the second half Carlisle began playing with Spurs which was a mistake, although a delight to watch as at times they became slightly casual. McGrath came on for Jones on the hour and he should have been on from the beginning. He at least had the confidence to hold the ball.

One felt sorry to see him in such a dismal side. Peters played one of his non-existent games, although he did make a few dummies which were meant for forwards who so patently were not there, unless he was hoping that the ball would run all the way to Gilzean in South Africa.

Spurs still seemed to be suffering from the Chivers phobia, even though he was not playing. Disjointed, hanging around, blaming each other. There are two ways to build a team – around a group of individuals, or, as Carlisle have done, around an idea. Even at the 60s' heights, Spurs owed their success to four of five brilliant individuals. Now, they have no one to pull them through.

Evans, Naylor and Beal continuously belted the ball pointlessly upfield, hoping that if they booted it far enough everyone would forget who had hit it. You would think the World Cup had never happened. Yesterday with not even one forward capable of fighting for the ball, the ball was simply endlessly given away.

Carlisle, never having any super stars, know that no one will do it for them except themselves. They have been brought up to work selflessly as a unit. After yesterday they are no longer a team to watch but a team being watched. Spurs alas, are now a team to watch. Watch them disintegrate. As for Carlisle. Keep humble. Just savour being in the First Division, for as long as it lasts.

Weather: Sunny. Ground: Firm.

Goal: Balderstone (20 min) 1–0.

Carlisle United (4–3–3): Ross; Carr, Winstanley, Green, Parker; O'Neill, Train, Balderstone; Martin, McIlmoyle (sub. 70 min. Clarke), Laidlaw.

Tottenham Hotspur (4–4–2): Jennings; Evans, Naylor, England, Beal; Coates, Pratt, Perryman, Peters; Jones (sub. 60 min. McGrath), Neighbour.

Referee: Roy Capey (Staffs).

English First Division: 24 August 1974
A Collector's Item

ARSENAL	(2)	4	0	(0)	MAN CITY
Kidd 2, Radford 2	27,143				
CARLISLE	(1)	1	0	(0)	TOTTENHAM
Balderstone (pen)	18,426				
COVENTRY	(0)	1	3	(1)	CHELSEA
Cross	21,251				Cooke, Garner, Locke
DERBY	(1)	2	0	(0)	SHEFF. UTD
Hector, Davis	23,088				
IPSWICH	(1)	2	0	(0)	BURNLEY
Talbot (pen), Whymark	22,324				
LEEDS	(0)	1	0	(0)	BIRMINGHAM
Clarke	30,820				
LIVERPOOL	(1)	2	1	(0)	LEICESTER
Lindsay, 2 pen	49,398				Weller
MIDDLESBRO	(1)	1	1	(0)	LUTON
Mills	24,579				Butlin
QPR	(0)	0	1	(0)	STOKE
	21,117				Hurst
WEST HAM	(0)	2	3	(2)	EVERTON
Bond pen, McDowell	22,486				Doyle (pen), Latchford, Harvey
WOLVES	(2)	4	2	(1)	NEWCASTLE
Hibbit 4 (1 pen)	23,526				Tudor 2

		HOME					AWAY				
	P	W	D	L	F	A	W	D	L	F	A	P
Carlisle	3	1	0	0	1	0	2	0	0	4	0	6
Ipswich	3	1	0	0	2	0	2	0	0	2	0	6
Liverpool	3	1	0	0	2	1	1	1	0	2	1	5
Wolves	3	1	1	0	4	2	1	0	0	2	1	5
Everton	3	1	1	0	2	1	1	0	0	3	2	5
Arsenal	3	1	0	1	4	1	1	0	0	1	0	4
Derby	3	1	1	0	3	1	0	1	0	0	0	4
Stoke	3	1	0	0	3	0	1	0	1	2	2	4
Manch City	3	2	0	0	5	0	0	0	1	0	4	4
Middlesbro	3	0	1	1	1	3	1	0	0	3	0	3
Chelsea	3	0	1	1	3	5	1	0	1	3	1	3
QPR	3	0	0	1	0	1	1	1	0	2	1	3
Newcastle	3	1	1	0	5	4	0	0	1	2	4	3
Leicester	3	0	0	1	0	1	1	0	1	5	5	2
Sheff. Utd	3	0	1	0	1	1	0	1	1	2	4	2
West Ham	3	1	0	1	4	3	0	0	1	0	4	2
Leeds	3	1	0	1	1	1	0	0	1	0	3	2
Burnley	3	0	0	1	1	2	0	1	1	3	5	1
Coventry	3	0	0	1	1	3	0	1	1	3	4	1
Luton	3	0	0	1	1	2	0	1	1	1	3	1
Birmingham	3	0	0	2	3	7	0	0	1	0	1	0
Tottenham	3	0	0	1	0	1	0	0	2	0	2	0

1978

Kevin Keegan

IT WAS a sunny afternoon in late autumn and the players were finishing off their second training session of the day. Hamburg's training ground is deep in the country, some 15 miles from the city. There were about 100 spectators, mostly children, straight out of school, plus a few families and old men with nothing to do. They were polite. The team's Yugoslav trainer had only to tell a photographer once to keep well back, and that was enough for everybody.

He gave them a final pep talk and the players then left the pitch, making their way up a long, tree-lined lane to the dressing rooms. The spectators allowed the players to pass unpestered – except for one, the smallest player in the group of 20. Every child wanted his autograph. They followed him up the lane, strung out behind him, politely taking turns for him to autograph their glossy scrapbooks or the backs of their T-shirts. He was like a diminutive Pied Piper, leading the children of Hamburg.

One girl had the whole of the Liverpool team embroidered down the back of her jacket. How strange that a child in the far north of West Germany should be so loyal to a foreign team. Even more surprising was the fact that Mr Keegan, an English footballer, should be speaking to them in German, a language he knew not a word of just over a year previously. It was pidgin German, with not much idea of grammar, but that wasn't stopping him. His wife Jean knows more German, having taken an A-level in it, back in Doncaster, but that seems to stop her speaking as freely as her husband – he bashes on regardless, refusing to use English even with those Germans who can speak it.

Most English footballers are very insular. They travel abroad but see nothing. They believe, with very little personal evidence, that their First Division is the best in the world. Their minds have been taken over from the age of 13 and processed to be footballers and led to believe that nothing else matters.

Keegan had just won the German Goal of the Month competition which unlike the British versions, where a studio panel decides, the voting is done by the public. He decided that for the first time he would be interviewed in German.

So far on German TV he'd used an interpreter. The crew turned up at his house next day and he dealt with all the questions most impressively.

As British footballers go, Kevin Keegan is most impressive. How many people, let alone footballers, would choose to shake up their whole career and their whole life just at the moment when they'd got to the top? This was what he did when he left Liverpool, the European champions, in 1977. He walked into trouble of almost every sort when he moved to Hamburg, but he's now come through it. The previous week, when playing away at Cologne, he'd been clapped off the pitch by the rival supporters.

Hamburg pay him a basic salary of £100,000 a year. The team was currently third in the league and his bonuses meant that altogether they must be paying him about £130,000 a year. After tax he takes home about £70,000. At Liverpool, as their big star, he got around £25,000 a year taking home £12,000.

His outside-football income is even greater – and it goes through his own companies based on the Isle of Man, with all the tax advantages. His annual income, from all sources, must by now be around £250,000. He is certainly on the way to becoming the first millionaire British footballer – if he hasn't already made it.

I asked an elderly German gentleman, who was watching the training, what he thought about Keegan. 'Ver goot player,' he said. 'And ver goot with this.' He made a rustling motion with his fingers. Keegan's salary has been all over the Hamburg papers, along with the other Hamburg players, showing him well ahead, which didn't help him much in the settling-down period.

The previous day Keegan had flown to Liverpool to take part in a testimonial match for Chris Lawler, playing for Swansea against a Liverpool team.

He'd paid his own way to Liverpool, and taken no expenses, and had gone despite a slight injury. He'd gone because he'd promised to go. Kevin doesn't let people down – one reason why the whole sponsorship of footballers in England is now on the increase again, recovering at last from the damage done by G. Best.

Bill Shankly, the former manager at Liverpool, was at the testimonial match and spoke to Keegan afterwards. 'Jesus Christ, you've climbed Everest, son . . .'. Keegan was naturally very pleased. 'Now see if you can stay there . . . .'.

Keegan was a late starter as a footballer. At secondary school in Doncaster, nobody encouraged him – in fact the sports master said he would never make a professional. It was a Catholic secondary school and he was in the grammar stream. He sat seven O-levels and passed two, Art and History. His father was a miner who had originally come from Durham, and before that the family had come from Ireland.

He started off as goalie for the school team but then was put on the wing as he was too small. He went for a trial with Doncaster Rovers, but when he turned up no one was there. Then he had a proper trial, lasting several days, for Coventry City, but they sent him home again. Jimmy Hill was manager at the time.

So at 16, armed with his two O-levels, he was forced to look for a job. He sat a little test to become a junior clerk in the storeroom of Peglers Brass Works ('Write all you know about a post box') which he passed and started on £5 a week. He was very scared of the factory girls. He had to go through a whole crowd of them on an assembly line and they promised him a special treat at Christmas. He discovered this meant being stripped and smeared with grease. Luckily, just before Christmas he was rescued from a fate worse than death by Scunthorpe United. He'd only made the reserve team at Peglers Brass Works, but they'd seen him in a pub team and offered to take him as an apprentice.

He started at Scunthorpe on £7, cleaning the lavatories, swept the terraces and ran the baths for the first team. It was at Scunthorpe he took up weight training and managed somehow to shoot up from 5ft., which he'd been at 15, to his present 5ft. 7in.

In the close season at Scunthorpe he took summer jobs, as many Fourth Division players still do, to supplement meagre wages, working in the local steel works or as a porter in a mental hospital. At home in Doncaster one September he first met Jean, now his wife, on the waltzer at the Leger fair. Her parents ran a local fish and chip shop and she was still at school studying for A-levels. He didn't tell her for many months that he was a footballer. He thought it might make him look flash, so he said he worked in the Scunthorpe steel works. It didn't make much impression when the truth came out: she didn't know that Scunthorpe had a football team.

By 1971, Keegan was 20 years old and had become a regular in the Scunthorpe first team. For a year there had been endless stories of big clubs coming to watch him, but nothing ever seemed to happen. The scouts were impressed by his buzzing around, but not much else. He seemed doomed to be a Fourth Division player for ever. 'Perhaps they thought I ran funny. I got very depressed and frustrated, and very bored. I even thought of quitting football and going back to Peglers.'

Then in May 1971 Bill Shankly signed him for £33,000. It was a modest sum, even for those days, but many people thought it was a lot for someone who'd been watched and then rejected by almost every other First Division club. He was offered £45 a week by Shankly, refused, asked for £50 and got it. Very cheeky.

He presumed Liverpool had bought him as reserve fodder, to be built up in the background for a few years, then perhaps given an odd game. It was the end of one season, so his arrival was hardly noticed, but by a series of lucky breaks – the first team forwards being out of form – he was given a chance the next season in the first team. The rest is Roy of the Rovers.

In six years with Liverpool, he won everything the game has to offer, starring in a team that dominated England and then Europe. In his autobiography, he was very honest about his own qualities: 'My game is completely centred on my work rate. I get involved for the full 90 minutes and receive the ball so much because I have an appetite for it. I do not look upon myself as a skilful player and never have done, no matter how much people have tried to convince me I am. I know that I have a degree of skill. I know what I can and cannot do. But if people use the expression "world class", I hope they do so because I know how to bring out the best in the players round me and therefore make a better player of myself.'

Watching him, perhaps the most remarkable thing, apart from his energy, is his heading ability. He can leap to enormous heights for a small man, a quality that was never properly used when he played on the wing for Scunthorpe. It still surprises defences round the world. He also thrives under very close marking, being able to survive and flourish against such heavies as Berti Vogts, Gerrnany's toughest defender, in the 1977 European Cup Final. (But he's not beyond retaliating, if he has to suffer persistent fouling, and he's been sent off four times in his career.)

All the same, there has been a doubt in many English minds that a lot of his bustling has not always bcen profitable, that he circles endlessly, often ending up further back than he began, his body almost at right angles to the ground, his tongue between his teeth, an over-excited little terrier in search of an opening. Perhaps this was the reason why the big European clubs were slow in coming, when he announced in early 1977 that he was in his last season with Liverpool.

Even now, he keeps coming back to the subject, almost as if explaining to himself the reasons. There had been no rows, no failures, no setbacks. Perhaps it might have been better if there had. As it was, all he'd had was success. Success can be very monotonous.

'I didn't enjoy the last year at Liverpool. In fact I think the year I liked best and the year I think we played the best football was the one year I was with them that we won nothing. I hope my lack of enjoyment didn't show. Only Jean knew how I felt. I still tried as hard, trained as hard. I just felt my game had grown stale. There were no more challenges. I'd achieved all my ambitions. I wasn't moving forward any more. I wasn't improving or developing as a footballer or as a person. What I had at Liverpool was a career. But what I wanted was adventure.

'In some ways I envied Cally (Ian Callaghan, the ex-Liverpool mid-field player) and respected the 800-odd games he'd played for Liverpool, settling for a life with one club, but to do that I'd have to wear blinkers. It wasn't me. I need constant challenges.'

So at the end of the season he went off to Hamburg SV who'd offered £500,000 for his services, not as large a sum as expected, but a record for the Bundesliga. There were cries of 'traitor!' from the Kop and even boos and hisses in the streets. Brian Clough attacked him while they were waiting to do a TV programme, criticising him for not supporting Britain. 'I asked him where he'd got his sun tan – and it was Spain of course. Only last week at London Airport a Scouse waiter came up to me and said he'd always liked me at Liverpool, but now he hated me for going to Hamburg. I let him finish, then asked him why he was in London. "Oh, I couldn't work in Liverpool. No money up there . . .". People are quick to see the faults in others but not in themselves. They'll move from Owen Owen to Boots for another fiver a week but hurl abuse at someone who moves from Liverpool to Man. United.

'In England, the Press and public build up superstars – only to knock them down. In the USA, they build people up – and then worship them. Funnily enough, I think I'm better liked in Britain now I've gone abroad. Coming to London as a Liverpool player, you'd expect criticism, being a Northern player. I'm now an England player who happens to work abroad.'

His reception on first arriving at Hamburg was incredible. Up to 4,000 people turned out each day in the first weeks, filling the leafy lanes of the training ground, just for a glimpse. He was immediately christened Machtig Maus – Mighty Mouse – a name which has still stuck. The Hamburg crowds now chant his name at matches in English "Kevin Keegan is the King. We all love him." They find Keegan easy enough to pronounce but stumble over Kevin which usually comes out as Ke-win. They handsomely won the pre-season matches, beating Barcelona (Cruyff included) 6-0. Then it all started to go wrong . . .

'It took me three months to realise that maybe I'd bitten off more than I could chew. I learned more about the politics of football in the first six months than I'd learned in the previous ten years. What I didn't know until I arrived was that I was the manager's last chance. He'd bought me to keep his job. He'd promised the club a superstar and I was what he'd been able to buy. Most people wanted him out. The local paper said he wanted to be both King and Pope, which about summed it up.

'On my first day, he asked me to come and do an hour's autograph signing. I had to do six hours, not realising it had been in the papers that I'd sign from 9 to 3. I came home furious, realising I'd been used, vowing I wouldn't get caught again.'

In Germany, as in many European countries, the manager is simply the figurehead, the business organiser. It's the trainer who has most to do with the players, coaching and picking the team. Keegan found himself caught in rows between the manager and the trainer, with each coming to him for advice, trying to get him on their side. 'The trainer had arrived at the same time as I did and he could speak English, which was one of the reasons he was given the job. He hoped I would back him against the manager. When I found out what was going on, I decided to sit on the fence and let them kill each other.'

Meanwhile, on the pitch, Keegan wasn't getting the ball. He felt resentment from some players, perhaps because of his salary and getting all the publicity. 'I thought my play was OK. I was trying as hard as I could. But it's not like being Bjorn Borg. You can only do so much on your own in football. It's a team game and you need everyone to help you. But the team seemed to be destroying itself. I'd fight to win the ball, give a one-two, but never get the ball back. I had to be greedy, which isn't my style of playing.

'I had no intention of returning to England, with my tail between my legs, but if some other foreign club had bid for me, I would have gone. I even stopped my Linguaphone lessons. I thought, what's the point of learning German, I won't be staying here . . .'

Then he was sent off, in a friendly match against Lubeck. He found he'd been suspended for eight weeks, and thought that would be the end. 'In a way it helped me. The team did badly when I was out and the crowds slumped. I think some of the players then realised they needed me. I got more of the ball when I returned as it was now a matter of staying in the *Bundesliga*.' In the end they finished the season tenth which wasn't good by Hamburg standards.

But the biggest change came when on the same day, within minutes of each other, the manager and the trainer both went. In came Gunther Netzer, the German World Cup star, as manager and a Jugoslav, Zebec, as trainer. Several players soon went and it was laid down in training that the style of play from now on was to feed Keegan. 'Netzer told me he would do this. It was like the sun rising. I couldn't believe it. You don't buy someone like me and not use them – you either play to their strengths or sell them. There's now a great spirit in the club.'

All this frustration and background rows will come as a surprise to the Hamburg fans. Throughout it all, Keegan continually said in the local papers how happy he was and publicly criticised nobody. Perhaps the frustrations were in his head ?

I talked to Horst Bertl, one of the Hamburg players, who is married to an American and speaks excellent English and is now Keegan's closest friend at the club. 'There were problems, on both sides. Hamburg people have a different mentality from the British. They're very cool, reserved, not very outgoing. Kevin moved into a house a long way away, which didn't help us in getting to know him. Perhaps one or two players didn't pass to him – but that happened to be their style, too. After all, we'd just won the European Cup Winners Cup when he arrived. He came as a world-famous star, so perhaps there was a feeling he'd be big-headed. Now we know he isn't. He's very down-to-earth. We all hope he'll stay. I personally want him to.'

Anyway, the footballing problems are apparently now over. Keegan himself thinks that he is playing the best football of his life – a fact reflected in his performance for England against Denmark, when he scored two goals, both with his head. (It was the first of these which had won him the German Goal of the Month competition.)

'I've been forced to develop and change my game, by the things going wrong and by the nature of the German game itself. Football is totally different over here. In England, games are won or lost in the midfield. That's where the struggle is, all in about a 40-yard stretch. In Germany, they surrender the midfield. They keep a spare man at the back, the libero, but everyone else waits and marks man to man. It means if you beat a man, you can have a 60 to 70 yard run in empty space before you reach the next man. I don't have to wheel round the way I did in England, looking for space.

'It's very much an individual game, you against your marker. I always have their best defender put against me, Vogts or Bonhof. Every week there's a big piece in every sports page of how this week I'm going to be marked out of the game. That's the sort of challenge I like. I don't do so much heading as I did at Liverpool. They don't put many long crosses into the box. I've had to learn to shield the ball more. We do more one-twos out here, double passing, or *Doppel Pass* as the Germans call it. I feel fitter than I've ever been. The new Yugoslav trainer is very tough.'

The training session looked much like an English session, with games of one-touch, keep ball, shooting exercises, heading, tackling, volley playing and then a proper practice match. The big difference is that they rarely do any training without the ball, and two days a week, Tuesdays and Thursdays, they have a morning, 9 to 10.30, and an afternoon, 4 to 5.30 session. In England, they train only in the morning.

On Fridays they also train in the afternoon, and then go straight into their training *Lager* or camp, not returning to their families until after Saturday's match. Home or away, they spend Friday nights at a sports hotel. (In England, teams rarely spend Friday nights together before a home match, the notable exception being Liverpool.) They have their evening meal together, are allowed one beer each and then must be in bed by 11. On Saturday morning they are all up by nine. In England, the tradition is to sleep in until mid-morning. At 11, they have their pre-match meal. In England, players are allowed some choice, depending on what they think suits them best. At Liverpool, Keegan always had fish. In Hamburg, the whole team is given veal steaks.

He's been told by the England team doctor that meat takes 24 hours to digest, whereas a bar of chocolate goes down in an hour. He eats the steak but just before kick-off, as he always used to do with Liverpool, he also has a bar of chocolate. He's convinced it gives him energy.

At 12 they have their team talk, which is about the same time as an English club. The blackboard comes out and they discuss final tactics.

At 12.15 they all go back to bed, putting on pyjamas and getting under the sheets till 1.30, though nobody appears actually to sleep. This is in complete contrast with England. This is the time, on away games, that English players sit in some smoke-filled hotel lounge, shouting obscenities at the football previews on the TV.

They have a 20-minute warm-up on the pitch before the match, a habit which is now creeping into British football. 'At Liverpool, players would stand in the dressing-room in their boots doing exercises, which was silly. Much better to get a feel of the ground, get a sweat going, then come back, put on a clean shirt and go out.' And as with all good football teams, they all shake hands before they finally enter the pitch.

Is it a harder league than England? Ah, well, depends what you mean by hard. There are only 18 teams in the German *Bundesliga* as opposed to 22 in England. This season, as Hamburg were knocked out in the first round of their Cup (and they only have one) Keegan will play only 35 competitive matches.

With Liverpool, his average was 60 to 70 a season. Hamburg don't have mid-week matches, which is one reason they do more training, but they do take part in a lot of friendly games. There is also a mid-season break at the height of winter, from mid-December to mid-January. So, in number of matches and length of season, the English league is more arduous. But from the footballing point of view, he thinks it's just as hard a league to win as in England. All 18 are good teams – there are no push-overs. The overall standard is much the same as England. 'Because it's a smaller league, all the teams have a hard season. In England, the season is over for some teams almost halfway through. A team like Coventry, say, at least over the last few seasons, often knows by Christmas that it's not going to be in the top six and get into Europe, nor will it be demoted, so the interest can often go. In Germany, you can win two points and jump five places, or lose and drop five places. Until almost the end of the season, the top half of nine have a chance for Europe and the bottom half can get demoted. It makes it much more competitive for every team, all the season. I prefer it that way. I think the English leagues have too many teams.'

He has to wear the team suit when staying at hotels, whereas at Liverpool they could wear jeans. The team wears Adidas equipment which led to some heated discussion when Keegan was seen to pull on a Patrick boot (made in France) before his first match. He'd just signed a £30,000-a-year contract to wear Patrick boots before Hamburg had come along, so naturally he wasn't going to change.

The club is sponsored by Hitachi, for which the club gets £150,000 a year, and it's strange to see them playing, in training or on Saturdays, with huge Hitachi signs on their chests, much bigger than would be allowed in England. Small boys wear Hitachi shirts like the players, as if the team was called Hitachi. In common usage, the team is called HSV – which comes from its full proper name, *Hamburger Sport Verein*.

Keegan has found, since going to Hamburg, that he's stopped swearing. It struck him when he went back to play in the testimonial that many British players swear with every second word. He doesn't swear at home with his wife, nor at work when he has to speak German, so the habit has almost gone.

'They play tricks on each other, as English players do, and we have some good laughs, but the humour is a bit different. In England, if you missed a ball in training someone might say to you, do you want a white stick. In Germany, they might possibly get hurt by such a remark and take it seriously.'

He was determined from the beginning to live the German way, not forever rushing back and forth to England, which was why he bought a house, rather than renting. During my visit, his wife Jean was about to have their first child – and it was going to be born in Hamburg. That was another thing Brian Clough had attacked him for. Surely he'd be flying her back to England to have it? No, he wanted to do the job properly. If he was playing for Hamburg, he would live like one of them. He doesn't have the English papers sent out, except a friend sends him the *Liverpool Echo*. The only thing they miss, apart from family and friends, is English TV. 'And Shredded Wheat,' added his wife.

They live in a very modern, flat-roofed bungalow about 24 miles from Hamburg, part of a new estate on the edge of an old village. The fields come right up to his living-room window. It's a Hollywood-style bungalow, with mammoth rooms and large pieces of furniture. It cost him £70,000. If he stays another year, which was in doubt, he thought he'd move perhaps to a £150,000 house, this time with a swimming pool.

Jean, his girl friend from his Doncaster days, has settled down well, but then she did have the advantage of that A-level German. She worked in a tax office in Liverpool before they got married in 1974. 'She's a clever girl, but rather shy and retiring. Coming to Germany has improved her. She's had to go out on her own to clinics and classes and get to know people.'

'I see more of Kevin here than I did in England,' says Jean. 'It's looked upon as a full-time job here, with training twice a day. In England when he finished at midday, he would spend afternoons opening shops and doing business and I hardly saw him. Here he just wants to relax in the evenings. We entertain more than we did at home. It was no use saying to him, during that last year at Liverpool, that he was just being silly, he should be glad to be in the best team. He doesn't moan or get bad tempered. He's just restless. He's such an ambitious person. He always wants to better himself.'

Keegan intends his next move to be Spain, either at the end of this season, or the next. It depends who comes along and how well Hamburg does, particularly if they get into Europe. At 27, he knows he has got one more chance to command a huge transfer fee, perhaps even a million pounds this time, and another enormous salary. It will have to be Spain, or perhaps Italy. 'You have to make it when you can. You never know what will happen. I might decide to retire with £250,000 saved but when I did, that £250,000 might be worth only 250,000 lire.'

His wife is rather more wary about Spain. She doesn't care for heat, being very light-skinned. She was pleased at the thought of Germany, but she doesn't know a word of Spanish. Kevin sees it all as yet one more wonderful challenge. 'I'm looking forward to learning Spanish. It will be the perfect time. The next World Cup is there – and I want to be playing for England. That's my greatest ambition. That and owning a horse which wins the St Leger in Doncaster, my home town. I'll be well known in the three countries by the time I finish. England, Germany and Spain, and I'll speak three languages. That can't be bad for the future.'

After two or three years in Spain, there then might be a final year in the USA. 'I wouldn't go now. I can't see Ron Greenwood picking any one from the American league.' Jean has worked out the time scale and reckons it should mean they will end up back in England just as the baby is starting school. He's promised he'll finish at the top, getting out in four or five years.

'I wouldn't like to know what I am going to do. That would spoil the surprise. If someone were to tell me that in five years I'll be managing Real Madrid, or Brentford, I wouldn't want to know. I just know that I'm a four-year man. That's the maximum I could ever stay anywhere. I've already been offered managerial jobs, but I wouldn't take them. I tell myself I don't want to go into management. I've spent all this time building up my name. I could lose it overnight. Look what happened to Bobby Charlton at Preston. But who knows what will happen. That's what's so exciting.'

His wife is not so excited at the thought of all the uncertainties and challenges and changes ahead. 'Now that he's started moving round the world, I often wonder when it will stop. Will he want to keep moving forever? Will he settle even when he's finished football? Will we ever come back to England . . . But I don't let these things worry me. To me, the most important thing is that we are together as a family. I'm happy to follow wherever Kev's boots take us.'

He drove me to Hamburg airport for the plane back to London. Almost every official seemed to know him, which isn't surprising as he spends half his life at the airport. As we passed a telephone box a man rushed out and grabbed him by the arm. 'Herr Keegan. You like speak with my daughter, ja?' I wondered for a moment if I'd chanced upon something indelicate, but he said it was a normal occurrence. People having telephone conversations are always breaking off to ask him to say a few words to the person at the other end. He gabbled down the line in German for a few moments, doing his party pieces, and then handed back the phone. Then he went back to his car, a stocky, muscle-bound Mighty Mouse, swinging his sports bag. It was an Adidas bag, the ones used by the rest of the team, but he'd put travel labels over the name.

One can do nice things for nothing, for English visitors or German fans, but one must protect one's sponsors.

1978

Vamos, Vamos Boys

Nottingham Forest 1 Tottenham Hotspur 1

WHO'D HAVE thunk that Spurs would so quickly be glamorous again. It looked during that final deadly match at Southampton last season that they were doomed to a second spell in the boring old Second Division. Yesterday, all eyes were on them. Today, at their open-day training session at Chesthunt, they expect 10,000 to turn up. The suede coats are reappearing as the hangers-on get ready for a fun-filled season. Yesterday's excellent performance will make a lot of difference. But it will take till Christmas for us to know how the Little Argentinian and the Big Argentinian can really cope.

A draw technically was a fair result, but it was a brilliant academic exercise, something I thought was well above them, considering all the scrambles we had to witness last season. Despite so many new players, new styles, new positions, they not only foiled Forest but infuriated them.

By the end the Forest crowd which started off by shouting 'Jesus Christ and Peter Taylor' or 'What a waste of money' was almost silenced. Both Villa and Ardiles were worth every penny and will be a threat to every First Division club. Almost every other Spurs player should also have a Ph D in the post.

Spurs were cool despite the setback of an early goal. Daines, carrying on as he often carried on last season, dropped an easy ball from Robertson and O'Neill was given two chances before knocking it in after 12 minutes. All the same, Spurs continued with their meticulous build-up. It might have looked Latin but in fact they did it all last season, or tried to. It led at last to a goal when Gorman, who had started hesitantly, intercepted and gave Moores acres of space to lumber at will through the Forest half before passing to Villa, who took his time before scoring.

In the second half either side could have scored, especially Withe who hit the bar and McAllister, who at least deserves house points for being in the opposing box. But he fell over an open goal after Villa had done all the hard work.

Forest were much tougher on Ardiles in the second half and managed to knock him off the ball several times but Villa they found impossible to stop.

They'd been calling Ardiles the Little Fellow behind his back in pre-season training, which was a bit rude, till one player asked, rather embarrassedly, if he'd had a nickname, back in the Argentine. 'Lalo,' he replied. None of the

89

present squad has O-level Spanish, so he was asked what it meant. 'Little Fellow,' so the Little Fellow replied.

As for Villa, they've been impressed by his big stomach muscles and his strength in training, but a bit worried about his somewhat lackadaisical approach to thoughts of the English First Division (the best in the world, and other lies). He'd smiled a lot, but that might have been lack of English.

Ardiles had caught them several times in training by his habit of appearing to lose the ball, only to make them look foolish, and by his equally smart habit of appearing to lose the conversation. 'Pass the salt,' they said to him over lunch. Ardiles passed the pepper. No, the salt, dum-dum. Ardiles passed his knife. One move ahead, you see, making them look foolish. These Latins.

Ardiles understands English remarkably well, but then he is a middle-class chap, son of a lawyer and halfway through his own legal training. (Does this make him the only middle-class born player in the First Division? Answers on a postcard please to Jimmy Hill, London, Wubbleyou Dubbleyou.)

The effect of their arrival has been interesting. There has naturally been some resentment, particularly from that clutch of ex-first-teamers playing yesterday in the reserves. A normal, native signing is given six weeks to make a mess. But when you've been baited from another planet, dripping with crowd appeal, and fresh from Argentina's vamos-vamos-go-go-success, you have to be given 12 weeks to be found out. (Plus extra time for culture shock.)

'It's made everyone that bit more competitive. Nobody wanted to look a mug in front of the new lads,' said one Spurs player. What with John Gorman returning from a long injury (never having really arrived, since coming from the Racing Club of Carlisle) and John Lacy being signed from Sporting Fulham, four players at least knew they were for the chop.

All it has taken, to make Spurs passing glamorous, is money. Keith Burkinshaw, a sensitive soul whom one hopes will never turn nasty to survive, well deserves his Manager of the Close Season Award, soon to be presented by Wincarnis.

'The style is definitely back at Tottenham,' said captain Steve Perryman, the veteran boy wonder. 'It reminds me of eight years or so ago when I'd just got in the first team, when there were big stars like Greaves and Gilzean, Jennings and Chivers, and we were winning things. Since then, we've had little glamour. Now, we've had huge crowds on tour and cameras everywhere – yet we haven't done anything yet. I hope it's not all premature . . . but I'm optimistic.'

On yesterday's show, Forest have already realised their peak. As for Spurs, the best looks yet to come. Definitely the best match of the season so far . . .

1980

Father Allen

UNLESS YOU'RE a football fan, you've probably never heard of Clive Allen. He's a young person of 19 and for the past few weeks he's been playing in the reserves for Crystal Palace, a South London team currently at the bottom of the First Division.

He became the first teenage million-pound footballer back in June, when he went from Queen's Park Rangers to Arsenal for £1.25 million. All of 62 days later, Arsenal transferred him to Palace, bringing his total transfer fees in just two months to £2.5 million, of which Master Clive's cut amounts to about £100,000. Now you remember him.

Even if you are a football fan, you probably know much more about Les Allen, his father. Exactly 20 years ago he was inside-left in the Spurs team of blessed memory, which won the League and FA Cup 'double,' and made sure that every living Spurs fan would die happy.

We've all seen price rises in 20 years. But can you really believe that in 1960, in the all-conquering Spurs team, Les Allen's wage was £20 a week? Today, someone like his young son is on £500 a week, while people at the top of the profession, as Les was, the stars like Kevin Keegan and Peter Shilton, earn at least £1,000 a week, just from football. And that can easily be doubled by outside engagements.

There were, of course, a few extras for Les. Let's not forget the £4 bonus for a win and £2 for a draw, and as Spurs won nearly everything that season he was often on £28 a week.

Les always wanted to be a footballer, but when he left Albert Street School, Dagenham in 1952, aged 15, there wasn't exactly a rush for his services. So he went to the local labour exchange and asked if they had any jobs in football. It sounds prehistoric, doesn't it? And they fixed him up, which is even wierder, getting him a trial for West Ham.

The trial led nowhere, so instead Les went into a factory to become an apprentice model-maker, and played for a local works team, Briggs Sports. They got into the semi-finals of the FA Amateur Cup in 1954, and the First Division scouts suddenly arrived on their bikes, offering young Les undreamt-of opportunities. He signed for Chelsea on £7 a week. He felt over the moon, or whatever it was footballers felt back in the mid-Fifties.

In 1959, he was transferred to Spurs, in exchange for another player,

Johnny Brooks, so no money was ever mentioned, nor did he get a signing-on fee. One day in February 1960, Spurs beat Crewe 13–2 in a Cup game before a crowd of 64,365. There hasn't been a bigger score in English football since then. Les Allen scored five.

In 1961, when the £20 maximum wage for footballers was abolished, Les did at last get on the gravy boat, going up to £65 by 1965 when he was transferred to QPR for £22,000. This was a record fee for Rangers, though Les, once again, got nothing.

Today, he works as a model-maker for a firm in Essex – he was sensible enough to finish his apprenticeship during his early years with Chelsea – having finally left football in 1974, when he was dismissed as manager of Swindon. He owns his own detached but modest house in Hornchurch, Essex, and has no regrets about his playing days. Nor is he jealous of the money his son's generation are earning.

'During that double year with Spurs, we got no extras, no one asked us to open shops and meet beauty queens. The best you could hope for was £10 for an article in the newspapers. I never even went to a night club.

'The only time I got a lump sum of money was for my benefit. In those days, if you served five years with the same club you got £750 – which came to about £450 after tax. I got that twice, at Chelsea and Spurs.

'I had a better life than the normal working man of the day, if only just. I was very happy and don't feel resentful. The only thing that often strikes me is where did all the money go to? At Spurs, we played to crowds of 55,000 every week, often twice a week. The players certainly didn't get the money. Who got it?'

Clive still lives at home with his parents, so Les has seen at first hand the changes in football, and he's not so happy about several of them: 'We're now ex-directory. We've had obscene calls, begging calls, cranks, the lot. My wife has been under a lot of strain, and so have I. People seem to think Clive is a millionaire. No one can now speak to him without permission from his club, but I can give you his agent's name . . . .'

Clive, being a modern young footballer, has all the usual accessories, such as lawyers and accountants to help with his financial and contractual affairs. A marketing firm has just put out a glossy brochure which shows him with a half-naked model draped round his shoulders, and says he is available for photographic sessions, promotional work, probably even barmitzvahs and masonic meetings.

Like his father, he is sensible and modest. He studied hard at his local comprehensive and got six O-levels, by which time his appearances for England Schoolboys had brought the scouts flocking, so he didn't have to bother with the labour exchange.

He drives a Ford Capri and has a regular girlfriend, a nurse, and he tries not to think about all the money he is supposed to be worth. Anyway, that's the least of his pressures. There are many drawbacks, you see, to being a modern footballer, with all that fame and fortune, which Les never had to face.

'I had no pressures off the pitch,' says Les. 'But I did have the pressure from the reserves. In those days, the top clubs had two good teams. If you weren't doing your business, a reserve would soon take over. Today, a star can play badly and still be in the first team.'

Clive played yesterday in Palace's first team, having been left out for several weeks. Recently it was rumoured that he could be on the move again, perhaps for another £1 million. Malcolm Allison has just taken over as manager, so anything could happen.

'That's been Clive's biggest problem of all,' says Les. 'The lad's life has been continually upset, yet he's only been a professional two years. I think he's now had eight different managers. No wonder he's not had time to settle down.'

Managers, of course, have seen their lives change somewhat in 20 years, usually exiting left, still holding telephone. In the three years since Clive joined Rangers at 16, he has worked for Dave Sexton, Alec Stock, Frank Sibley, Steve Burtenshaw, Tommy Docherty (twice), Terry Neill, Terry Venables, Ernie Walley and, at the last quick look in the manager's office, Malcolm Allison.

'People say, well, at least he's got his £100,000. That's all pie in the sky,' says Les. 'He hasn't seen any of it yet. It's spread out over the future years, and mostly goes towards a pension. He never talks or thinks about the money. He just wants to play football. It'll be there of course at the end of his career, a nice lump to finish with. That's more than I ever got . . . .'

1980

Wembley Way

I STOOD in front of the Royal Box, raised the cup aloft and with the roars of 100,000 cheering fans ringing in my ears I gave the victory salute. Then I did it again. I'd noticed that the photographer hadn't been quite ready. I wanted my day at Wembley immortalised for ever.

Pure fan-tasy: H. Davies holds aloft the Cup at Wembley Stadium

The noise seemed even louder this time and I felt a lump in my throat and completely over the moon as I waved wildly to the Wembley terraces. I hope the photo's a good 'un. I've sent off my £3.45 to Wembley Tours Ltd and they say it should be back in about ten days. Full colour. None of your rubbish.

It's Jake's birthday soon and I'm planning a terrific outing for him. Whether or not Spurs get to Wembley for the Cup Final, and as I sit here, reporting from my desk in my room at the back of the house, the semi-final against Wolves is yet to be played, I've decided to treat him with the next best thing. A tour of Wembley Stadium.

You didn't know there were such things? I didn't know either. We have a painter in the house at the moment, Stuart, who's doing our hall, lovely paper, bought from Cole's and I don't know the price yet as it's being kept from me but wait till the cheque comes back and I know I'll have a fit. Anyway, Stuart's been round Wembley three times and swears it's brilliant.

Jake is very critical these days. Well they all are, those teenagers. Bloody cynical, never a word of praise or even 'fanks, so I thought I'd try out the treat on my own first of all, give it the Father's Day seal of approval. I advise all parents to make a note of it. A bargain at £1.50, 90p for children, on the hour almost every day.

I only hope the photograph comes out OK. As long as it's not too wide a shot. I don't want it to be too obvious that I'm waving my arms ecstatically to an absolutely empty stadium. That could really ruin the image.

The tour lasts about an hour and ten minutes and you start with a talk from a guide on the history of Wembley and the FA. Our guide seemed very knowledgeable, considering she was a Dutch girl speaking English with an American accent. Then there's a little film show with great sound effects, showing the highlights of various sporting events at Wembley over the years.

Perhaps the best bit is going into the dressing room, yes the actual dressing-room, where they have the strips all laid out, as if for a match. They also have some historic shirts on display. I touched the shirt worn by Nobby Stiles when England won the World Cup at Wembley in 1966. I don't think I'll wash my hands ever again.

The *really* good bit is going from the dressing room into the tunnel. It's more of a bus shelter than a tunnel, big enough to take two double-deckers. You're made to wait there, splitting into two lines, like they do before a real match.

There were about 50 people on the tour I joined last week, a rainy Monday at two o'clock, not even school holidays. Where do they all come from, all the lonely people? At a signal, you all move forward and then suddenly, just as at last you spot the brilliantly green turf, the noise of 100,000 cheering people welcomes you out on to the pitch. They have known people to faint with the emotion of it all.

I took so long ogling the pitch that I got separated from my party as they set off round the greyhound track which surrounds the pitch. It's a hanging offence if you dare put one foot on the turf itself. I stumbled into the Royal Retiring room by mistake, trying to find them, and I'm now privy to what goes on in there. My slips are sealed.

I caught them all up as each one in turn was climbing the 39 steps to the top of the Royal Box to be photographed holding up a large silver Cup. Not the real one, though I'm sure it will look genuine in the photograph. At £3.75, it had better be. That's quite expensive, now I think about it, but then you don't think, do you, not when you're carried away by all that Nuremberg excitement coming out of the loudspeaker.

They've only been running these tours for four years yet they now get 100,000 people going round every year. Amazing. Just to look at an empty stadium. Course, part of our heritage, innit. Taste of Britain. Who won the war then, I mean the World Cup.

I couldn't keep it a secret from Jake for long. You don't know what you're getting for your birthday, ha ha ha. I know and you don't. OK, it's an outing and you can take five friends, but only if you're very very good and kind to me. Here's a clue. You go round the North Circular to a place beginning with a Wuh. Then he guessed. Who wants to go there? You can see it all on the tele. Sounds boring.

I dunno. No soul, this younger generation.

W. H. HIRST. H. BEARDSELL.   G. ROBSON.   J. H. SUGDEN.
    J. S. THORP.   N. ROBINSON.   J. T. GENT.   J. SPITTLE.
        W. A. TOLSON.   S. GRIST.   L. SMITH. W. ADDELSEE.

Photo by Collins.   Huddersfield.
    N. McCASKIE.   R. B. HOPKINSON.   V. B. SYKES. W. S. THORP.
                HUDDERSFIELD (A).

1981

The Wright Way

IT WAS a Wednesday in November when England played Hungary that first, fateful time, back in 1953, and the match was at Wembley, just as it will be next Wednesday. This time it will be an evening match. In 1953, it took place in the afternoon. Floodlighting had not come in.

Billy Wright, who was captain that day, has gone through life ever since with people constantly reminding him of what happened. As if he needs it. He can recite, word for word, Geoffrey Green's description of the game in *The Times*, and he does so quite frequently in after-dinner speeches. It always brings the house down, so he says, especially the bit about Wright 'coming in for the intended tackle like a fire engine going to the wrong fire'. Puskas then sold him a dummy, pulled the ball back with the sole of his boot, and scored a brilliant goal, while W. Wright was still on his backside.

He can take it in good humour today, but at the time, wow, it was the end of the world. England's humiliation was all the more terrible for being so utterly and completely unexpected. England had ruled for so long, give or take an occasional upset at the hands of those Scottish fanatics. It was assumed that it was our game which no foreigners could ever hope to play better.

Now, what did he have for breakfast that morning in 1953? Must have been eggs and bacon. Billy always had that. Then it was eggs on toast for lunch, followed by rice pudding. 'We were staying at Hendon Hall Hotel, I think, and they knew how much I loved rice pudding. All the team used to joke about it. "Here's Wrighty's pudding." Yes, I was called Wrighty by then. When I was younger, I was called Snowy. I used to put on masses of sugar as I believed it gave me extra energy.'

He tied his own laces that day which was something he rarely did. In all his hundreds of games for Wolves, someone else, usually Johnny Hancock, tied them for him, one of his little superstitions.

The reason why he can remember few other of the peripheral details of that day was that it was just another international match. When you've played for England 105 times, and been captain 90 times, all the games run into one another. 'It was a normal match, not like playing against Scotland. That was never a normal match. You always rolled up your sleeves for Scotland.

'We'd *heard* of the Hungarians, as they'd won the Olympic Games in 1952, but we knew nothing about them, or their tactics. Nobody was interested in tactics, not in those days. Walter Winterbottom had never seen them play. We got a report a few days before that they'd beaten a French team 10–0, but that didn't worry us either. We'd never heard of the team they'd beaten.

'By God, it just took us a minute to realise what we were up against. The winger went down the wing and crossed on the run and Hidgekuti had scored before Merrick in goal had moved. Their ability was unbelievable. I've never seen such football since.'

Hungary won 6–3, as even today's schoolboys know, the first time in the history of the Universe that England had been beaten at home by a foreign side.

'We played them again next year, 1954, in blooming Budapest and got hammered 7–1. What a runaround they gave us. We were all sweating like the cobblers. It must have been 93 degrees. What I remember of that match is Ron Stanniforth taking off his boots after the game and saying, "No bugger touch these, they're red hot." '

It is pointless conjecture to wonder how the Hungarians would fare today, though one he is asked all the time. He thinks they would still appear a magical team. 'It was an excellent game. It's easy to forget that we had a good team out that day, Matthews and Mortensen, and that we did score three goals. Nine goals in a game meant one every nine minutes. The crowd cheered the Hungarians for their attacking display, but we were an attacking teams as well in those days. England played with two wingers, Matthews and Finney, and so did the Hungarians, so there was lots of excitement and thrills. There was none of these square balls or passing back you get today.

'Football today is at a crisis point and something will have to be done to bring the crowds back. Families don't come because of the hooliganism and secondly, there's not the excitement. It's all tactics, negative play which has taken the fun out of football. I watched a schoolboy match the other day, kids of eight to ten, and the master was coaching them how to play the offside trap. Such things were never talked about at all in my day, even when I became a professional.'

He joined Wolves in 1938 on 30 shillings a week as a boot boy. He came from Ironbridge, Shropshire, where his father was an iron moulder, determined that his son should never have to do such a dirty job. Young Billy was not a natural, which he is the first to admit, and was sent home when they thought he would never make it, but he returned and worked hard to improve himself. He finished playing for Wolves in 1959, on a salary of £20 a week, having won everything and been everywhere (he played in 43 different countries) and met everyone (tea with Rab Butler in London, Gigli shown up to his hotel room in Johannesburg).

From 1962 to 1966 he managed Arsenal, which ended in tears and failure, and he never returned to football management. He doesn't regret it, as it taught him a lot about life, and himself. He used to be physically sick with the worry of it all. 'I expected all footballers to be like me – prepared to give themselves 100 per cent for the team. They're not, of course. They're like people in most walks of life. Some are more concerned with money, or other interests.'

It's strange that none of our three most successful England players, Bobby Moore, Bobby Charlton and Wright, each with over 100 caps, has made it as a manager. Physically, there are resemblances, being fair-haired and stocky. Temperamentally, they always appeared calm, gentle people, at least off the pitch. 'I suppose we have similar outlooks. You've got to have a different sort of strength to be a manager, to be stern. Ruthless is, I suppose, the word I want. When you've always been at the top, everything seems to go for you, you don't have to be tough. When you stop playing, it's a different world.'

Billy Wright went on to create a career for himself in a different sphere, one where the failure rate can be just as high as football management. In 1966, only a day after he was sacked by Arsenal, he joined ATV in Birmingham in their sport department, appearing, then producing, and finally becoming the Head of Sports. His wife Joy admits she has been impressed at how well he has done as an administrator. 'He must have hidden talents,' she says. 'He hasn't got them in the garden. I have to force him out. The other day, I was watching from the window and I saw him drive the car to the front gate in order to open it ....'

'Oh, that's not true, Joy,' he said, but he could hardly get a word in, as she was then off, talking about his trophies which litter the house. She is clearly proud of them, but finds them hard to clean. 'The cups go all rusty. You polish them, and they're just as bad in two months.' His England caps are now in a plastic sack in the spare room, though he says they're going up again when they've decorated.

Everbody who was alive in the 1950s will not only remember Billy, the Golden Boy of Football, but the sensation caused by his marriage to glamorous Joy of the Beverley Sisters. Few thought it would last, the solid, but rather slow and worthy football player getting mixed up with the flashy world of showbusiness. Twenty-three years later, it is obviously a happy and lively marriage.

They met when she came to do a show in Wolverhampton. Her 11-year-old son Vincent was a mad football fan and wanted to meet Billy and see his trophies. A mutual friend introduced them. It must be nice to have your Mum marry your hero. (Young Vince is still a football fan – and works on *The Times* sports pages.) They have two girls, Vicky and Babette, who are now 22 and 17 and who have just started a showbusiness career. Along with their cousin Sasha, daughter of Joy's sister Teddie, they have a singing trio called The Girls. For a charity performance recently, all six Beverleys – the three Mums and three daughters – sang together. Billy and Joy have a house with a large garden in Hertfordshire. He also has a flat in Birmingham where he spends part of each week on his TV work.

He is a fit if rather hefty-looking 57-year-old today, weighing 13½ stone, a stone more than his playing days. He doesn't smoke and has recently given up sugar, at long last, at his wife's insistence. He is just over five foot eight inches, smaller in real life than he ever appeared on the pitch, which is what people are always telling him. 'I was always good at jumping.' As a player, one of his hobbies was making rugs. Back in the 1950s, time used to hang heavily for young professionals, before all this marketing and promotion. Now his main hobby is golf. His hair has lost its blondness and is now grey. It is fairly thick, though his wife teases him that he is losing bits of it. 'When he's washing his hair,' she says, 'I pull the curls over to one side and say to him, "Use the Empty Spaces!" '

'I am depressed about England's football these days,' says Billy. 'We haven't got the individual talent. Ray Clemence and Shilton, and Kevin, that's about all our real stars, but other countries are in just as bad a state. In my time, every country had two or three Maradonas. Now nobody has got those sort of world stars any more. Brazil hasn't. Germany hasn't. I put it down again to tactics. They're everywhere, not allowing the individual to project himself.

'I'm a great fan of Bryan Robson. I think he's the best midfield player in the country. He will be good for English football. The best thing for English football is of course the England team doing well.'

Mr. H. S. WILLMOTT.   W. PURVES.   J. ROACH   E. JOLLY.   T. COTTERELL.   C. SIMMS.
F. MOBLYE.   J. JONES.   W. OLLIS.   G. F. WHELDON.   H. HAYNES.
Photo by Reinhold Thiele & Co.
J. HALLAM.   T. HANDS
SMALL HEATH.

1982

Bryan Robson

THE MINUTE England had qualified for the World Cup finals in Spain, the people who like to pick Ron Greenwood's team for him, of whom there are 20 million, immediately pencilled in the name of B. Robson for next June. After all, he was the only player who had appeared in each of England's eight World Cup qualifying matches. In the past two years he has been England's most consistent player and about the only one not to suffer the personal abuse which was thrown at the team in that period.

That, plus the fact that he is the country's costliest player would, you might have thought, have made him a household name, if not a household face. Yet few people outside the game have heard of him. Even among the football faithful up and down the terraces, it is probably only the followers of Manchester United and West Bromwich Albion who could tell you very much about him. It is as if he had got to the top in disguise, coming through on the wings, so silently that nobody realised.

The *lumpen*-mass of professional footballers, toiling away every Saturday afternoon in our 92 league clubs, know they could never be Kevin Keegan even in their wildest dreams. They haven't got the German for a start – or his gift of the gab, or his skills, or his workrate in the television studios. But in their more realistic reveries they could possibly be Bryan Robson.

While Kev is an exotic, Bryan Robson is the archetypal English player, perhaps the best example of what our native game thinks it is all about, the very model of a modern member of the team.

On the pitch, he's never flash. He's not the star who catches the eye like Hoddle or Brooking, whose skills are obvious for all to see, but the solid core every manager admires.

Off the pitch he's equally unobtrusive, quiet, softly spoken, rather hesitant and unsophisticated, with none of Keegan's social graces – although he has picked up bits of the outward camouflage accepted by all star players these days, such as a gold bracelet, two rings and a gold chain. Could this be the influence of Ron Atkinson, his manager at Manchester United and West Bromwich and a friend to all jewellers?

'No. That was my wife, not Ron. She bought all the jewellery for me.'

He met his wife Denise at a local pub in Birmingham six years ago. She was having her 21st birthday party, so he bought her a drink, when he heard she was 21. 'It wasn't really like me, chatting up a strange bird.' She was a typist, but had her own car which was handy, since he hadn't. Nor could he drive at the time.

They have a 16-month-old daughter Claire and a second child due in June, about the same time as the Princess of Wales's, and as the World Cup. They are house-hunting in Cheshire at the moment, looking for something in the £100,000 range. They fancy something Georgian; 1982 Georgian, of course.

His background is almost an Identikit version of the English player. If you were making up his life, writing it like painting by numbers, where would you have him born? The North East, of course, where so many of our football greats have come from.

He was born in Chester-le-Street, County Durham, on 11 January 1957. His father is a long-distance lorry driver who these days spends a lot of his time abroad, lugging juggernauts through France and Italy. Bryan was christened Bryan, because his father was already Brian. He has an older sister Susan and two younger brothers, Gary, 18, now with West Bromwich, and Justin, 16, now with Newcastle.

He lived for Newcastle United as a boy. On Saturdays, when his father was at home, he and his sister Susan were taken to St James's Park, queuing up outside even before the gates opened at one o'clock. Bryan was very small as a child and his dad liked to get him settled on a wall, at the front of the terrace in the Wing Paddock, before the crowds arrived. In the Sixties, Newcastle were still getting 30–40,000 gates.

He collected programmes and hung team pennants on the bedroom wall of his council house, read *Tiger* and *Roy of the Rovers*, just like everyone else. He went to a comprehensive school at Birtley where, he says, he was quite good and liked history and geography, and if football had not come along he likes to think he could have got a few O-levels.

Football did not come along with a rush. He got into the district team, playing for Chester-le-Street, but never made the County team, let alone the English schoolboy team. (This again is typical: few who play for England schoolboys ever last the pace and become top professionals.)

He was very disappointed at the time not to play for Durham: he was captain of his district team, which included four boys who did get into the County team. Looking back, it could have been his smallness – or perhaps local politics, certain schoolmasters favouring certain schools.

One night when he was 13 there was a knock at the door of his council house and a gentleman was standing there who said he was a scout for the Burnley football club.

'Me Mam and Dad couldn't understand him. They didn't know what scouts were. It was a bit of a shock, like.'

The scout had been that day to watch Bryan's school team play another school team because he had been tipped off about the other team's goalie. The goalie had turned out useless, but he had been impressed by B. Robson and got his home address – they were not on the phone – from a teacher. It led, during his next school holidays, to a week's trial at Burnley, which he didn't really enjoy. He was put in digs, with one other boy, but left to his own devices, having to find his own way to the ground and back each day for training. The afternoons he whiled away on the putting green in the local park or at the pictures or just hanging about feeling lost. He couldn't understand the local *patois*, nor could they understand him. He would ask for a 'Coäk' in a caff, and they wouldn't know what he was on about.

Not long afterwards other scouts from other clubs started contacting him. He thinks the word must have got around that he'd been to Burnley (then in the First Division) so they all had a second look, even the ones who might have dismissed him earlier.

He was invited to West Bromwich for a similar week's training – but this time he loved everything about it. 'They just seemed to look after us better. It was all organised. All the lads were put in a hotel together and a mini bus picked us up, took us to the ground and brought us back. Our dinner would be fixed for us and we'd be given tickets for a match, if there was one in Birmingham that night, or the pictures. Nothing seemed too much trouble for them. They kept you involved.'

By the time he was 15 and able to leave school, four clubs had given him some sort of trial (Burnley, West Bromwich, Coventry and Newcastle) and 11 in all had expressed some sort of interest; but from his first visit to West Bromwich, he had decided they were the club he liked best and he told other clubs accordingly. 'I could have gone on trials to many other places, and I think now I should have done. That's what I've told my younger brothers. Until you actually sign for one, go everywhere.'

He was given no extra inducement at 15 to sign apprenticeship forms for West Bromwich, which again is probably typical (although in some cases underhand payments, or gifts to parents, do occur). The only perk from any club was from Newcastle United, who regularly sent his father free tickets for their matches, even after Bryan had told them he preferred West Bromwich.

The day he travelled through to Birmingham with his parents to sign the official forms turned out to be a bit of an anti-climax. 'They told me, just before I signed, that Newcastle had been on the phone and would still have me if I wanted to go. They said it was up to me. I couldn't believe it. It was as if they weren't bothered whether I signed or not. But I said, oh no, I wanted to come to them, so they said fine, sign here.'

When he arrived at West Bromwich in 1972 he was only 5ft. 2in. and weighed just seven stone. That was the main reason why nobody, least of all West Bromwich, had been exactly panting for his signature, although they all admired his skills.

'It was West Bromwich's chief scout, Paddy Ryan, who used to cheer me up when I got depressed. "I've seen your Mam and Dad," he used to tell me, "and they're normal height. You'll be OK." '

All the same, for the whole of that first year at West Bromwich he hardly played any football. He got his £6 a week as an apprentice, swept up the dressing-rooms and cleaned the first team's boots in the time honoured way, but he was given little chance to play football.

'It was for my own good, I suppose. They didn't want me knocked about by some big lads. I played only about 15 games in the whole year. I was in digs on my own, which is what I wanted. If you share with some other lad then every evening it's "What shall *we* do, where shall *we* go?" I wanted just to be on my own, make up my own mind what to do. But I was very homesick.'

At the ground, during training sessions, he was given lots of weight exercises to do. In his digs, his landlady was instructed to build him up, as if preparing a fighting cock.

'Every morning for a whole year I had a raw egg with milk, sherry, and sugar mixed in. It tasted awful at first but I got used to it. It was just the sight of the raw egg that put me off. Then every evening, after my tea, I had to drink a bottle of Mackeson. It was strange. I'd never tasted beer before.'

It must have worked – or something must have worked, if only his Mam and Dad's genes. Today, he is a tough and fit-looking 5ft. 11in., weighs 11 stone and is known for the fierceness of his tackling.

On his first game in the Reserves, away to Everton, he got bounced so hard by Bob Latchford that he ended up on the cinder track, a mass of cuts and bruises. 'No, I didn't say anything to him. He was a star. I was only 16.'

He didn't have a lot of confidence during the next season or so and there were various changes of management at West Bromwich, which didn't help. But the worst blow to his progress from the Reserves into the first team came in the 1976–77 season when he broke his leg not once but three times.

'It happened first against Tottenham, when Chris Jones kicked me as I was tackling him. It wasn't his fault. I came back too quickly, in just eight weeks, and on my first match back, in a Reserve game, I fractured the same leg in the same place.' He recovered from that, but just towards the end of the season, against Manchester City, he broke his other leg and was out for 15 weeks.

'I lost about a year in all before I was back to peak fitness. It didn't affect me psychologically. I never go into a tackle thinking I might get hurt again. The worst part was that it happened before I established myself. When you're established, and you get injured, everybody is waiting for your return and you get your place back quickly. But when you've never been there, you just get forgotten. You've lost all that time.'

It was the arrival of Ron Atkinson as manager in 1978 which confirmed him in the first team. He became a regular for the next three years and also played for the England Under-21 and Under-23 teams. When Ron Atkinson moved on to Manchester United, in the summer of 1981, Bryan Robson soon followed him, after a saga chronicled in the sports pages for weeks, with accusations from West Bromwich that he was letting them down, unsettling the team, and the papers saying he was being greedy.

'I'd been there eight years and I felt I needed a change. They didn't seem to me to be thinking of themselves as a big club. When good players like Stapleton or Francis were for sale, you never heard of West Bromwich making offers. I wanted a big club with big ideas.'

There was also talk of personality differences between him and the new West Bromwich manager, Ronnie Allen, but Bryan will say nothing about this. He has never been one for giving public opinions. 'I don't like people slagging each other off. I don't believe in criticising others. I just want to get on with my own job.'

West Bromwich asked £2 million at first and finally settled on £1.5 million – plus 15 per cent VAT and 5 per cent to the FA pension fund. Players no longer get a cut of transfer fees, but they do arrange their own terms and wages, helped, in Bryan's case, by an accountant and lawyer. 'I let them get on with it. While they went through the forms, I went for my medical. The price was ridiculous. We shouldn't have got to that state. No footballer is worth that sort of money.'

Other players have suffered with big prices on their heads. Steve Daley, perhaps the best known recent example, seemed almost to be diminished once he went to Manchester City for a record £1 million.

'I did have Steve Daley at the back of my mind when I went to Manchester, but I was determined to dismiss all thoughts of the money. I told myself it was nothing at all to do with me. I hadn't set it. It was the two clubs, not me.

'Instead I thought of what the pressures must be like for a striker who has cost over a million. As a midfield player, I felt no real pressures. I can go 20 games without scoring, and nobody will get at me.'

Since Robson's arrival Manchester United have greatly improved, shooting up the league. But he doesn't feel he is quite into his stride yet. At West Bromwich, in his last two years, he averaged, by his own standards, four good games out of five. In his first ten for Manchester United, he felt only three were good, one poor, and the rest average.

'It's hard to explain why a footballer sometimes doesn't play well. Nobody ever wants to play badly. Every professional always tries hard, whatever the critics might say.

'Some days it's because you're trying too hard. You rush in, play too quickly, make a mistake and your confidence can go. You have to steady yourself, slow down, read the game. Some days your touch is just not on. Then you have to say: "Well, I can still help the team, I can still run and still defend." '

He gets very upset by those who call today's footballers greedy. It wasn't the money that was the main attraction of Manchester United, whatever the West Bromwich fans (the ones who sent him hate letters) might have thought. In the end, his old club offered him a contract for five years which in basic terms was not far from United's.

'It seems that everyone in life can go out and work hard, earn as much money as they can to give their family a better life – except footballers. When it happens to them people call them greedy. Pop stars, golfers, tennis players, they get real fortunes compared with footballers, yet nobody accuses them in newspapers of being greedy.'

What happens, of course, is that disaffected managers, who have either lost or failed to get a star player, turn round in their ghosted columns and accuse players of holding them over a barrel.

The first and obvious difference between West Bromwich and Manchester United is the crowds. Home and away, if you play for United, you play to huge crowds who cheer you, regardless, all through the match. At West Bromwich, Bryan got ten to 12 fan letters a week. Overnight, after arriving in Manchester, the mail has jumped to 100 a week, from all over the world: Tahiti to Norway, Canada to Sweden. He answers all of them. He doesn't mind the postage, which he pays himself, but sending signed photographs is proving expensive.

Then there are the facilities. Some of them might seem rather trivial, but even after three months, Bryan could still hardly get over them. 'Do you know we get flip-flops and dressing-gowns provided by the club? Really. The training ground is terrific. At West Bromwich you just got changed, went home, and that was it. Here, after training, we can have a sauna, then we can put on our flip-flops and dressing-gowns and just wander round, casual like. There's a restaurant and a place where you can sit and talk to people, friends or the press. On the team coach they provide a real meal, you know. Steak and roast potatoes I had last week. We never had that on the team coach at West Bromwich. And there's a video. I get a free club car, a Granada 2.8 Ghia. It's really good. And every time you go to Old Trafford, no matter what time of day, there's always a sort of buzz. You really feel you're at a big club.'

He felt he played well in his first England game, against Eire, but was upset to be left out of the vital European match against Italy. 'I'd had an ankle injury. I tried hard in Australia with the England team to impress Ron Greenwood that I was better, but he didn't pick me. I watched the lads on television before the Italian game. They'd had tea with Mrs Thatcher at Downing Street and I felt really sick that I wasn't one of them as I saw them all coming out. It really hardened my attitude. I realised you can't take anything for granted.'

Since he returned to the team, he has remained – and has now got 14 caps and played ten games on the trot. Everyone tells him he is now a fixture, definite for Spain, but he refuses to accept it. He says he has to keep turning it on every week to keep his place.

The rituals with the England team are completely different from normal league matches. For a start, he has never seen Ron Greenwood give a specific team talk. 'He spends the time the England team are together picking off players individually and going through their specific jobs at a personal level. There's a relaxed, almost casual approach, but nothing is left to chance.' Even the chosen team is given out rather informally while the players are in tracksuits at training.

'I find it easier playing for England than in a normal league match. There's an extra spark, pulling on an England shirt, unlike the Saturday week in, week out, sort of game. I find I get more space. The opposition in internationals allow you more time than in League matches. Physically it's easier. But it's harder to get the ball back once you lose it.

'If we'd lost the Hungary match, we would have been lynched. I'm not kidding. We would have had to hide for four years, or emigrated.'

For England, he has been playing mostly in the middle of the midfield, which is where he prefers to play and where he played at West Bromwich. In the Manchester United team he has been operating on the left of the middle, leaving Ray Wilkins to be the middle man, which has taken him some time to adjust to. He is naturally left-footed, which helps. He has also operated very effectively as a sweeper for England which he thinks is an asset and hopes will give him a better chance of keeping his England place. In the years ahead, when his legs tire, he sees himself going permanently into the defence.

His main rival for England defensive mid-field position is his club colleague, Ray Wilkins. Brooking, Hoddle and Devonshire are really competing among themselves to be the mid-field creative man. Robson does create chances, and is at his best when going forward having won the ball in a tackle, and then surging past his man; but his combination of strong defensive tackling (which Brooking, Hoddle and Devonshire don't possess) and his eagerness to go forward when the chance presents itself makes him an almost perfect team player, able to help at the front and the rear.

Robson is an admirer of Ray Wilkins and hopes they both get into the England squad for Spain. They have been rooming together at Manchester on several occasions, but so far Bryan has not made a regular partner. At West Bromwich he always shared in hotels with Alistair Robertson. Footballers are very fond of regular habits. Robson feels lost if he isn't wearing a Number 7 shirt for Manchester United. That was always his number at West Bromwich, too.

His other bit of superstition is a champagne cork with a two pence piece on top, fixed in the wire, which he takes to every match. This started two years ago when he was first picked for England and a friend, an Italian who runs a restaurant, poured out champagne to celebrate, then gave him the top for good luck.

He firmly believes that England will do well in Spain, distinguishing themselves and quietening their many critics. 'Spain is a world stage and it's what several of our players need. Keegan is already a world player but I predict that both Trevor (Francis) and Glenn (Hoddle) will be known to the whole world after Spain. I also hope that Derek Statham (from West Bromwich) will come through between now and June and get his chance for England. He's a terrific player.'

Meanwhile, the weekly slog at Manchester goes on, battling to do well in the League and stay near the top. Perhaps his main slog is in the background. Like most players new to a team and a town, he became a displaced person, based in an hotel – the Post House on the M6, north of Manchester, where Atkinson himself stayed when he moved up. Bryan's family was left in Birmingham.

Despite his high salary in Manchester he says he has no capital apart from his Birmingham house, which is on a mortgage. 'If it all finished today, I would be on the dole. I'd probably end up back in a council house, where it all began.'

He is now determined to promote himself a little bit more, to take advantage of his new and glamorous position in the football world. But is he up to it? Doesn't it need charisma, Robbo? (His team mates either call him Robbo or Pop, after another footballer called Brian Robson.)

'Kevin and Trevor are more famous because they've been on TV so much. I have been nervous doing the occasional TV show. I'm not as bubbly as Kevin. I don't ooze his sort of confidence. But I don't see why it won't come. Just takes experience. I've done *Crackerjack* this week. That went very well. I enjoyed it.

'I don't like being flashy or living an extravagant life. I'm not really an individual player. I always think what's best for my team-mates, but I do want to do more things now. I want to do charity things, help children particularly. If you get close to the top you have a sort of duty to help the less fortunate.'

He then went off to book an appointment to have his hair done. He was due for another perm. It is not as distinctive a perm as Mr Keegan's, more a subdued version. But there again, Mr Robson is a more subdued person. But a very worthy one. I'd have him in my team.

1982

Going to the Match

SATURDAY AFTERNOON and we leave for the match as always about one forty-five having ruined the family lunch by bolting it and rushing to the TV to see the same goals we have seen several times this week already, if not this decade. I always drive the same route getting caught in the same traffic jams I've been caught in every second Saturday for the last 20 years. The cars have changed but the shop windows hardly at all. I stare blankly into funeral parlours, dodgy book shops, scrag-end butcher's which are always about to close for the weekend. I am convinced I can see the same left-over life I first saw in 1961 when I was on the way to see J. Greaves. I did try to vary my route once, to avoid some traffic lights, but ended up lost. It's now like following an emotional paper chase, signs on the passing faces, reflections in the windows, all clues that I've left for myself over two decades.

We always park in the same place. It's about ten streets away from the ground, but I know better than to try to get nearer. Going to a British football match is an obstacle race. The whole object is to repel you, to make it as hard and uncomfortable as possible. Only the daft and the dopey try to get near.

Thirty thousand, I say to 16-year-old Jake as I lock the car door. No, hang about, make that 34,000.

Every week, the same ritual. He refuses to play, so it's my own game. I have this theory that I can tell by the number of cars parked in this little side street at the same time every Saturday how many will be inside the ground.

We walk the same old route from the car, heading straight for the High Road, then up it, but take a different one back, to avoid the hooligans. I always buy a programme from the same bloke. He didn't seem to be there last Saturday. Could he be ill? Dead? No, there he is. Outside the supporters' shop. He's moved his pitch. How strange. I want to ask him why, but Jake growls me on, convinced we must hurry or we won't get in. That's his ritual, every week. I think it was in 1967 that I last didn't get into a Spurs match.

The smells are revolting. Would any sensible person dare to buy those hamburgers being poked into life by that scruffy lad? The most unshaven-looking stall-holder has his own black and white TV on the counter. We avoid beer bellies tumbling out of the pub on the corner, and then the young lads selling newspapers with a Spurs player on the front, in full colour, which is a cover for some left-wing organ and is even more boring to read than the

110

Old Spurs: team of 1953. Note Bill Nicholson, back row, far left,
next to Alf Ramsey

Spurs programme. The newspaper posters announce who is here from the
Daily Mail and the *Daily Express*. They all have such podgy faces. The
Biggest Voice in Sport, says one. Alas, the Biggest Drunk is not here today. In
provincial towns, the local posters boast that Joe Soap is here, from the
Evening Scream, neither of which you've heard of.

We have a seat today. This season, my post-cartilage legs are too weak to
stand in all that crowd, which means sending away three weeks ahead.
Today's tickets got lost. I sent away for tickets for two matches, which of
course completely confounded their booking system. Spurs must be the worst
club in Britain for getting tickets. All it took was a day on the phone trying to
get through. Have you ever tried to ring a football club and speak to someone?
You might as well try and get MI5, or a North Thames Gas Board showroom.

'When I was a lad, Jake, following Carlisle United, there was never any
trouble getting tickets. Or phoning up. You could get through to the manager
personally, ask him what time the match starts, and he'd say what time can
you get here.' Old joke. Jake doesn't smile. He really wants to stand on The
Shelf with the hooligans and looks upon supporters who sit as not true
supporters.

It's a rotten seat, right in the corner, with two pillars in front of us, but to
our right we do get a good view of the new and wonderful Main Stand going
up. It's been an eerie experience, watching such a chunk of North London
history being rased to the ground. The new thing does look quite pretty. I
can watch reflections of the players in the glass when they take throw-ins.

I share out the apples and the chewing gum and wipe my specs for the 16th time. I don't bring my whisky flask with me till the first Saturday in November. I have my rules. Jake says Brian Moore is here from ITV, but I rub my specs for the 17th time and still can't even see the cameras. Back in the Sixties, when the world was young, I wore my eyes naked to football matches.

The sound system in the North Stand, where we're sitting, is diabolical. All that money on their glass boxes, yet we can't hear a bleeding thing. What I want to hear is the name of the Forest sub. We have already recognised every Spurs player out there in the kick-around. I used to get confused now and again by Peter Taylor, Steve Perryman and John Pratt, if they all fell down together in a heap, as their hair and physique were very similar, but Taylor and Pratt have gone. It can take only one match for most footballers' body movements to be lodged in your brain, identifiable for ever.

Thirty thousand pairs of eyes are watching carefully, missing nothing. I often look around at a football crowd, examining the sea of faces, and nobody ever stands out, yet we can all focus out there on the pitch on one part of the one body, and see everything. I wonder if Desmond Morris is here today.

I failed to observe Brian Clough walking to his seat, just to see what scruffy old sweat shirt he might be wearing, perhaps even if he's still got his slippers on. Clough's style is lack of style. I don't think it's affected. What do you think, Jake? Oh, shut up, Hunt. I don't want any more talking during the match, OK, keep your opinions to yourself.

I dunno. You struggle to bring them up, a companion for your middle age, and they don't want the benefit of one's lifetime's clichés.

The best part in the first half was booing Kenny Burns. He had a bit of a tussle with Steve Archibald, currently the home crowd's golden boy, despite not having scored all season. 'We'll take good care of you, Arch-i-bald, Archy-ba-ald.' Rival supporters always jeer Hoddle, if he gets too clever, but that's just jealousy.

The act of booing Burns paid off, poor lad, because he then started giving the ball away and miskicking. Who says crowds can't affect play? Justin Fashanu got a few jeers when he started falling over, but as he was never in the game we all forgot him. I worried about Robertson. I felt he could skin Perryman down the flank whenever he wanted, and then leave Miller and Roberts for dead, but luckily he didn't often want to. What an awkward team Forest are at the moment. They seem in awe of Robertson, moving out of the way when he approaches. Their only plan was to give him the ball. Despite his brilliance, he was making their team lopsided. They played better when later he was taken off. I think he'll go, what do you think, Jake? Sorry, I forgot.

We were ahead by one goal at half time, so we sat still, feeling pleased. Anyone who might want to go to the lavatory or get a drink should not go to football matches. It's not just the squalor, which is disgusting, but the queues, usually full of Scandinavians. You can hardly get moving for them these days at Spurs or Arsenal home matches.

They come on cheap weekend returns from Norway and Sweden. While the wives go to Oxford Street, the blokes come to Spurs, weighed down with blue and white rosettes and badges. They also think it's part of the wonderful English ritual to have Bovril at half time. It means that for the whole of the second half they stagger back, blocking your view, muttering apologies like something out of an Ingmar Bergman film.

The second half was terrific. Hoddle and Ardiles took over the game and Hazzard, who'd started quietly, scored a brilliant goal. We hammered them, three nil. That was twice in a week we'd won 3-0. I don't think that's ever happened before. I must look up my old diaries. I've kept the score for every Spurs match I've been to in 20 years, along with the weather.

The crowd was shouting 'We're going to win the League' which wasn't as silly or as wildly optimistic as it might sound. It was the first time in over ten years that it felt possible. God, the struggles and awful performances and terrible defences we Spurs supporters have had to suffer in the last ten years. Those sterile but noisy Second Division games during which we clawed our way back. All muscle and little mind.

Next Saturday, I'll take it all back, when they play like dummies, but it was great to rush into the High Road afterwards and feel proud and pleased, seeing faces beaming, then smiles all round as the Arsenal news came through. (Beaten by Notts County, ha ha ha.)

I shouldn't really run, with my bad knee, but it's absolutely vital to get back to the car by five o'clock and hear that beloved signature tune of *Sports Report*. It brings back a thousand Saturdays, right from my boyhood. As the team had won I even smiled at Stuart Hall's match report. When it's a bad day, I groan out loud at him.

We always drive home in silence, listening to every crumb about every game. After the two Wembley Cup Final games, Jake said he wouldn't watch Spurs any more. He didn't expect them to reach such heights, ever again, not in his lifetime. Nothing will compare with that replay when Villa scored.

This season, Spurs are giving pleasure, thanks mainly to Hoddle, even if it all eventually collapses. Yes, still pessimistic. I suppose even Liverpool fans, deep down, half expect the worse to happen, just as Carlisle United fans half expect the best to happen. That's football. That's life. Just take one match, one day, one life, at a time, Jimmy.

1982

Super Spurs?

I WENT on a tour of Spurs' new stand last week and kept thinking about Disraeli. Football these days is Two Nations. Nowhere can you see it more clearly than at Tottenham Hotspur.

The imbalance amongst clubs is well publicised. Some are going bankrupt while others can spend £1m on one player. The difference between the players' lives is equally great. Glen Hoddle, aged 24, lives in his own house and can earn £50,000 a year from football. Down in the Fourth Division some of his fellow professionals are struggling on £5,000 a year, hoping for part-time work to pay the rent.

But the contrast in how fans are treated is less well known. Even inside the same club, the differences are astonishing. Last Saturday I queued for an hour to get into Spurs, then stood in squalor, exposed to the elements.

No fan has any moans when the team is doing well. Most real fans prefer to stand shoulder to shoulder in the primitive terraces, part of the cheers and the jeers, sharing communally in the excitement. We would like a bit more loving, a little more attention paid to our basic needs, but most of us do not want to be hermetically sealed behind plate glass windows, watching the match in our own padded box.

That is the way the game is going, at least at the top end of the market. Spurs' new stand is the most modern, the most luxurious in Britain. Clubs who have created new stands and installed luxury boxes include Manchester United, Coventry City, Nottingham Forest, Aston Villa, West Bromwich Albion, Queen's Park Rangers, Leicester City, Fulham and Orient. All of them, so they say, needed to create these special boxes, and get in some vital 'up-front' money, otherwise they could not have built a new stand in the first place.

If you hurry, there are still some boxes at Spurs still for sale. At only £30,000 each. For this price, you can have an eight-seater box for the next three years for you and your friends, or your clients. You can sit in a gold armchair and have the use of a cocktail cabinet, fridge, small kitchen and your own hostess. Each of the 72 boxes also has its own phone and colour TV.

Drink and meals cost extra, about £9 for a four-course lunch served in your box. You can also use the boxholders' lounge which is about the same size and style as the reception area of a medium sized Hilton hotel.

Tottenham Hotspur Football & Athletic Company, Ltd.

Official Programme

And Record of the Club.

Issued every Match Day. **PRICE ONE PENNY.**

Vol. IV. No. 39. MARCH 23, 1912.

COCKY (Reporting from Coastguard Station): Saturday, March 16. Steamship Liverpool struck on the Spurs' Rock at 5 p.m., and became a total wreck. Valuable cargo saved. Ship touching bottom; doubtful if she can be raised.—COCKY.

C. Coventry Trade Union Printer, Lower Tottenham.

As I was standing in an outer office, waiting to talk to the Spurs commercial manager Mike Lewis, there was a call from the Dorchester Hotel to say that an Arab Prince wanted a box for Saturday. It's Manchester City tomorrow, not the very best of the season's attractions, so a box for that match is only £550. The scale, for a one-off match, goes from £475 to £600.

'We've sold 34 out of the 72 boxes so far,' said Mr Lewis. 'I think that's a better record than any other club at the time of their opening.'

The Spurs' new stand was officially opened two weeks ago, when the ceremony was performed by Sir Stanley Rous. Mostly big companies have paid out the required £30,000, on the nail, and they include Barclays Bank, Beecham's Foods, National Giro, Mecca and Tesco, all of whom have their name plates on the entrance hall. Last week, a local pub, the Railway Tavern, also got their name up, just for one match, for £600. One firm, Brown and Jackson, surprised them all by buying a 21-year lease on a box. They see it as an investment.

Mr Lewis has seen for himself how the other half lives in football. He comes from Newport and after several years as a fund-raiser for children's charities he joined his local club in 1976, his first job in football, to try to help them from going bankrupt.

'My first job at Newport was to go and get a ball for the lads to play with. They'd painted up all the old balls so often they were beginning to look like rugby balls. The refs used to look at our ball on a match day, give a wink, and pass it as new for the match itself. They knew we couldn't afford anything better.'

No sports shop in Newport would help because the club had run up so many debts. 'I had to go to Ebbw Vale, and find a shop who didn't know about us,' Mr Lewis said.

When Mr Lewis arrived as commercial manager four years ago, Spurs' income from sponsorship, lotteries, etc., was £40,000. This year they should earn £1.1m. A club which can pull in that sort of money must have a healthy future.

When poor old Chelsea invested their all in a brave new stand, the team collapsed. By sheer coincidence, the present Spurs team is their most attractive and most successful of any in the last 15 years. Think what a white elephant that £4.5m stand could have been.

The club now has two shops just outside the ground, full of souvenirs for the fans. This year they will make a £50,000 profit on a £380,000 turnover. The club has recently begun its own travel agency, in which football trips play only a secondary part. Lotteries, advertising and sponsorship made £282,000 last year.

For one part of the football nation, there's a lot of money around. If a team is successful.

1982

Ron Greenwood, England Manager

RON GREENWOOD is a very popular gentleman. It would be hard to find anyone who didn't like him as a person. He is good company, an excellent talker, warm and thoughtful, intelligent, kind and considerate. Is he a good manager?

Alf Ramsey was hard to like. A conversation with him was an endurance test, sticking it out, hoping that he might actually say something. He was admired by those close to him, so they said, but to the world at large he was taciturn, cold, sullen, suspicious.

Don Revie was feared, suspected, and then actively disliked, though for a long time the mutterings were muted. An England manager, after all, has a lot of power, many gifts to bestow. Few people in football, whether press, players or officials, want to cross such an important personage.

Greenwood arrived like Jimmy Carter, the good clean guy that everyone desperately wanted, after all the murk and mud. It was probably partly his niceness that got Greenwood the job in 1977, rather than ten years previously when he had also been in line.

If England had failed to qualify for Spain, today Greenwood would be a remote figure from the past, pensioned off and forgotten, sitting about the seafront at Brighton, the Man who Let Us Down. Nice bloke really, but not up to the job. Let's try that loudmouth Clough.

Ron Greenwood was born on 11 November 1921, in the village of Worsthorn near Burnley in Lancashire. His father was a painter and decorator and when the depression hit Lancashire in the Thirties he moved south with his family, taking Ron and his sister to Alperton in North London, not far from Wembley Stadium. Ron was ten when they arrived, with a strong Lancashire accent. 'I did have the Michael taken at school.' There's no trace of it today. He is the complete suburban Londoner.

At 14, he left Alperton Secondary School and became an apprentice sign-writer, rather than just an ordinary painter, as he had shown artistic tendencies. Over the next five years, he did some work inside Wembley Stadium. He painted the words 'Gents' and 'Exit', amongst other things. They're probably still there. Wembley Stadium is a mausoleum of our times.

He played in various London youth teams and played two games for Chelsea's first team before being called up into the RAF. For two years, he was stationed in Belfast and played for Belfast Celtic as a guest player, the only Englishman on their books. Later he was stationed in Bradford and played for Bradford Park Avenue, along with Len Shackleton.

After the war, Bradford formally transferred him from Chelsea for the sum of £3,000, a record fee for Bradford. He was in and out of the team and it wasn't until 1949, when they sold him to Brentford, that he returned to London and blossomed as a strong and thoughtful centre-half and a responsible captain. In 1952 he moved back to Chelsea, winning a championship medal with them in 1955, before rounding off his playing career with a year at Fulham, along with Jimmy Hill and Bobby Robson, finally retiring as a player in 1956, aged 35.

'I continued my career so late, well after 30, so I'm always careful today never to dismiss players when they get over thirty.'

It was a reasonable, solid career, without being spectacular. He managed to make one appearance for the England B team and in 1954 he was named in the squad of 40 for the World Cup in Switzerland, but never made the party which went.

While he was still at Chelsea, he became coach for the Oxford University team. He had his FA coaching badge by then, one of the first to get it. 'I was petrified at the thought of telling students what to do. I pointed to my badge, and said it was new, and that I was still learning and that I hoped we would all learn together. It was a very happy and constructive time for me and I learned a lot. While we practised, on the next track, Bannister and Brasher and Chataway were training to break the mile.'

His first job as a manager was at Eastbourne United, where he spent nine months. He moved to Arsenal in 1958 as assistant manager and then to West Ham in April 1961, only the fourth manager in the club's history. For the next 15 years, he guided many players who later became eminent coaches and managers. He is still very proud, justifiably, of his three West Ham products, Moore, Hurst and Peters, who played such a vital part in England's 1966 victory.

The next stage in his football life is strange and rather confusing. In 1975 he voluntarily kicked himself upstairs and became general manager, handing over the West Ham team to John Lyall. 'Without ever telling young John, I had seen him for a long time as a natural successor, even when I first took him on as a wages clerk, and then youth coach. I felt I owed it to West Ham to ensure suitable succession. I felt, in my wisdom, that it was time after 15 years to give up. I nearly got the sack as I'd forgotten to tell the board before I'd told the players and it leaked out to the press.'

They were slightly upset, but getting the sack would have been an exaggeration. Greenwood, in his whole life, has never had the sack, a boast which few managers today can make. Nor has he ever had a contract. Always the gentleman, right to the end.

He and his wife Lucy bought a house at Brighton, ready for their retirement, and at 55 looked forward to seeing more of their grandchildren. For the next two years, he felt completely displaced. He was doing a little bit of scouting for West Ham, in his supposed role as general manager, but not much else.

'John used to tell me to get more involved, to take part in training, but I felt it wouldn't be right. I suppose I took it to extremes and kept right away. I soon realized that I was missing the everyday involvement I'd had for so long.' So from 1975 to 1977 he did virtually nothing, except slowly begin to suffer for his own decision. 'It was a period of shutting myself away. Pure masochism. I had punished myself. It was nobody's fault.'

There is little doubt that the real reason for this retreat was the state of football. He won't discuss it, being too kind and diplomatic, but he seems to have suffered an almost Wordsworthian wave of disgust at what was happening to the game he so dearly loved and had given a lifetime to improve. The world is so much with us. Getting and spending, we lay waste our powers.

There is little need to go into the fall of Revie, and the way in which he fled to the Arabs, but for a period it did look to many purists as if everything in English football had become underhand, obsessed by money, the means justifying the end, while the rise in power of the merchandising men was beginning to rival that of the managers. Perhaps the saddest part of the Revie regime was that many players had become less than keen to play for England, especially at Wembley.

The England call came in September 1977, and surprised many people. Greenwood had been with the England camp before and had taken over the Under 23 team in 1958 when Bill Nicholson became manager of Spurs. But that job had finished in 1961 when he went to West Ham. He was by now almost 56, rather old to rally the lads, or so it was thought by many people.

Out of his first 30 games as England manager, the team won 20 and suffered only three defeats, a fine record, though with hindsight it can be seen that most of the wins were against greatly inferior teams. (With hinder sight, those at least were the days when we *could* beat inferior teams. Norway had yet to happen.)

It was the European Nations Cup in Italy which found England wanting, left behind by other countries, lacking in skilled players, about which little can be done, but unable to blend together the few that we did have. Greenwood appeared to have relied too heavily on Keegan who, for various reasons, was not at his best.

Greenwood has tried out 43 players in the last four years. Of the youngsters who have come through the Under 21 and Under 23 teams (and Greenwood must be praised for making them proper staging posts – and for giving these teams high quality coaches and managers) only two so far have graduated through to senior level and properly established themselves. They are Robson and Sansom. Hoddle has as yet not made it, and we have yet to know what Greenwood thinks about him and whether he will be given a further chance before June. Even with Sansom, Greenwood appears to have had occasional second thoughts and dropped him after the Switzerland defeat. Robson is his only definite success, a young player found and carefully nurtured to full English status.

He has also been very unlucky with injuries. In the last two years, there have been serious accidents, at vital times, to Keegan, Brooking, Francis and Thompson which have meant drastic changes. The worst Greenwood can remember was against Brazil last season. Nineteen names had been announced, but on the Thursday before the Saturday match, only ten turned up. The rest were injured, or being treated. 'They were dropping like flies.'

Given all these problems, and the continued criticism which every England manager has to suffer once he has been in the job for more than a year, it doesn't sound a load of fun for a 60-year-old grandad, not when his retirement home at Brighton is beckoning. He lives there already, but drives up to London in his Rover, after he has taken his wife her early morning cup of tea in bed at seven-thirty.

Greenwood was sitting in his rather small office at the FA's London headquarters in Lancaster Gate, almost bare except for a photograph of England's 1977 squad and a large year planner pinned to the wall behind his back. He looked slightly tireder than in his West Ham days, and was carrying a bit too much weight with all the travelling round the world and attending too many functions.

'What problems? There are no problems about being England manager. It is a pleasure and an honour to be able to deal with the cream of the country's players. There have been only four managers in the history of the England team. When I think how humbly I started in life, I now sit here, equally humbly I hope, and I'm aware that I have achieved something by being England manager.

'There are low moments which are different from the low moments in being a club manager. At a club, you can knuckle down every Monday morning and try to *do* something about it. There's little you can actually *do* as England manager.

'It's a very lonely job, the loneliest in football. You lead a strange life, very isolated in so many ways.

'But I have never not enjoyed it, even at the worst moments for the team. I like to think I'm more affable as England manager than I was at West Ham. At West Ham, some people did accuse me of being truculent and difficult. That was because at West Ham I was not on my own. I was representing the whole club, defending people who could not otherwise do so. When West Ham was unfairly attacked, or any member of it, then I did get angry and answered back. With England, I am on my own. I make my own decisions and am responsible to no one. I can just sit back and enjoy it.'

He does of course still answer back, now and again, and can be sharp at press conferences, just as he can be tougher in private with players and his staff than might appear from his public image. His fluent tongue can bite rather sharply. His closest colleagues at the FA have noticed that it is in

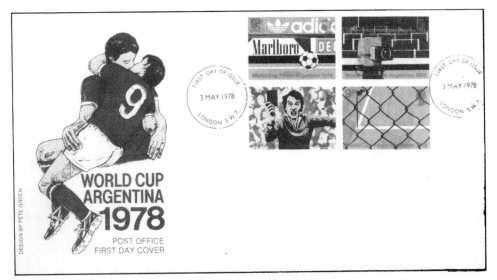

World Cup cover, 1978: study it carefully – it's not quite the official one . . .

victory, rather than defeat, that he can be at his spikiest. It is as if the security of a win makes him speak his mind and put the critics in their place. In defeat, he is humble, accepts the blame, smiling, if a trifle wearily. Hasn't it made him rather cynical, this endless round, one minute the hero, the next the villain?

'I am very philosophical. The press and the public only relate to the facts, they see every match as joy or misery, as ups and downs, they don't look at the background, at what is really happening. Every member of the public is entitled to his opinion, and that's how it should be.'

He keeps no bulky dossiers, the way Revie did, though he might make the occasional note on a likely new player. Most of what he knows and thinks is in his head. 'I am looking for players who can improvise and adapt. That is the secret of a successful representative player, rather than a club player. You can't be rigid and set down patterns. They only meet for a few days, and then don't see each other for perhaps three months. You've got to be flexible. The last thing they want is a set of instructions on how to play.

'I have never used a blackboard in my life, despite what some people might think. My whole philosophy of football depends on one basic idea. It is a simple game. Let's not complicate it.'

Newcomers to the England team are also surprised that Greenwood dispenses with any formal team talk. Before League games, the normal club manager gets his lads together in some smoke-filled hotel lounge, making them sit still and pay attention, while he goes through their tactics and duties, giving warning and guidance. Greenwood has none of this. He prefers to talk to players individually and informally, usually while training, taking them aside for little chats.

121

'Their attention strays in team talks, and there's little need for them anyway. With a one-to-one relationship you have their full attention, talking about their particular needs. They are supposed to be the cream, when they're picked for England. You don't need to try to teach them things.'

He doesn't day-dream about his perfect team, so he says, nor does he wake up at night with a new inspiration, pencilling in a new name in his all-star team to take on the world. He has schooled himself *never* to have an ideal team in his head at any one time. It would be too depressing. Until they all turn up, fit and well, on the Thursday before the match, he will never decide on his final eleven.

'I've only once since I've been England manager changed my mind at the last minute, after I'd decided on someone.' He won't name the player, naturally enough, but from the conversation at the time, which was about how he gathers the team at their hotel before a match, it looks as if it was simply a player's nervousness, how he was behaving with the rest of the party, which made him have second thoughts.

'I have always tried to be loyal to players whom I believe in. I played Ray Wilkins, for example, when he was playing badly for Chelsea, because I believed in him. I believe in loyalty to sound players who are experienced in the England squad. I always talk about the squad, by the way, never the team. I see the squad as what matters, the family unit, in which everyone is equal.

'I am willing to stick with someone in the squad, who has had squad experience and I know can be trusted, rather than a player outside the squad who might at that moment be playing better. But I tell them all – you are now in the squad, stick in and you'll stay in.'

Has he made mistakes, any he would admit to publicly? He thought for a bit and then said that in Italy he should have decided finally between Clemence and Shilton, announcing once and for all who was number one. Then he rather took it back, saying it wasn't a mistake, not in the sense perhaps I had meant.

He revealed that by June in Spain, he will have ceased to alternate them in goal. Injury, or loss or form, could of course change his decision, but it would be clear at last who was England's number one goalkeeper.

'I feel very sorry for young players when things go against them. Rix, Hoddle and Sansom have each had bad games, when nothing seemed to go for them. I told them so, that I was sorry for them.'

Then why didn't he stick by them, if he still believed in their basic skills?

'Previous performances can have a bad effect on players psychologically. Some find it hard to shake off their disappointments. The effect boomerangs. They have to be strong-minded, and I have to know which are the ones who will be strong.'

He is very much looking forward to the World Cup in Spain, the ultimate experience for any national manager, though he is still far from pleased about the way the team got there.

'If we are determined and play to our strengths, then we have a good chance. I think we should get through the first group, and then who knows? It depends who we are drawn against.

'I was asked the other day by a foreign journalist who I was responsible to. I said nobody. I am responsible to no one. Then I thought a bit. Responsible to no one, except the nation . . .'

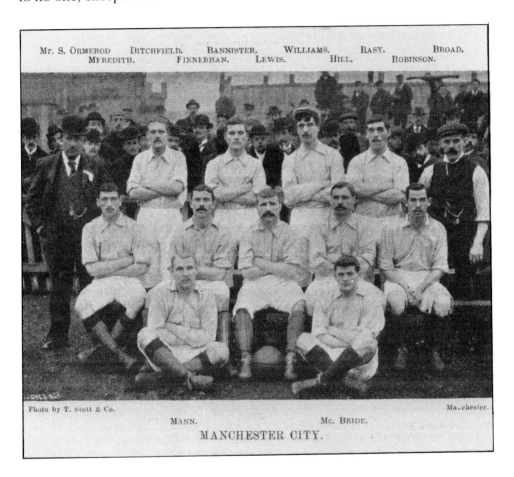

Mr. S. Ormerod   Ditchfield.   Bannister.   Williams.   Rasy.   Broad.
Meredith.   Finnerhan.   Lewis.   Hill.   Robinson.

Photo by T. Stott & Co.   Manchester.

Mann.   Mc. Bride.

MANCHESTER CITY.

1982

The England Doctor

RON GREENWOOD went out to Spain over Christmas, to have a look at possible training grounds and likely hotels. The FA party which will fly out in June will contain around 50 people, so a lot of arrangements have to be made.

Not long afterwards, Dr Vernon Edwards was also making plans to catch a plane to Spain where the water flows mainly in the pipes. He wanted to bring back a sample, and also some of the bottled variety, in order to have them tested by a local laboratory in sunny Watford and, with a bit of luck, pronounce it perfectly all right. You have to be very careful, when you're looking after a party of 50 people, especially when 22 of them are supposed to be in the peak of physical condition. You don't want any of them to be as sick as Spanish parrots.

Dr Edwards is the club doctor at Watford FC, and also club doctor for the England team. He went to Merchant Taylors' School and St Thomas's Hospital, started as a GP in Watford in 1956 and is now, at 53, the oldest partner in a partnership of six.

He became club doctor at Watford in 1963 when they were stuck for someone to look after the injured. They had heard that Doc Edwards was a hearty sort of chap, just finished an active rugby career, terribly keen on squash. In 1970 he was asked by Alf Ramsey to doctor to the England Youth team.

He went with them to the Little World Cup finals in Czechoslovakia and came up against his first real injury crisis. Trevor Francis, then 16, ran into the goal net, grabbed at it and pulled the crossbar down on top of himself. 'I thought he'd fractured his thigh, but he had damaged only his musculator. I mixed up some plaster of Paris in my hotel bedroom and put him in it straight away. This was somewhere in East Czechoslovakia, can't remember the name of the town, miles out of the way. I'd taken the plaster bandages with my medical kit, just in case. We got him fit in just one week, fit enough to play in the final against Portugal. And we won!'

Today, Dr Edwards has a hotel napkin signed by all those Under 18 players on the wall of his Watford surgery, along with other England photographs and team badges. It's not to show off but to distract young patients. He finds it a good talking point if children are a bit nervous.

He progressed to doctoring the Under 23 team, now disbanded, then the

Under 21 and B team, and in 1978, on the death of the then England first-team doctor, Peter Burrows, he was appointed the England doctor. Just like the players, you have to work your way through the ranks. By then, of course, he already knew most of the stars, having followed them up from the Youth Team.

Like all the England officials, from the manager to the kitman he sees himself as part of the family, changing into a training suit for all England games, including their training sessions, and willing to do anything that's necessary. 'I carry the bags if needed, pick up the shitty clothes from the floor or put in stitches. After I've washed my hands, of course.'

He has a check list for Spain, which he has used on all England's tours so far, but doesn't expect too many unusual problems. Spain is used to English tourists, so he doesn't expect any difficulties with the food (which he is also in charge of), but he'll probably take out an assortment of English breakfast cereals, tea bags, chocolates and sweets, so they don't feel too far away from home. The mental problems could be more difficult. Assuming the team does well, they could be out there for up to 29 days, which is a long time to be away from their wives and girlfriends.

'It is a problem for young healthy athletes, but polar explorers can manage to do without, and round-the-world yachtsmen, and Everest climbers, so I think for the sake of England, and the biggest event in their careers, they can manage a period of abstinence . . .'

In Spain, one of his duties will be to supervise their afternoon rests, which they always have on the afternoon before an evening match. You don't necessarily have to sleep, though most do, but you have to stay in your room. Dr Edwards makes sure their phones are stopped, with no out-going or in-coming calls to waken them.

Between matches, the big problem will be boredom. The manager usually tries to organize various activities, if possible. Footballers never care for sightseeing, no matter where they are, so that's out. Golf is more in their line, or swimming, though he doesn't like anybody swimming too strenuously, as that uses, and can abuse, different muscles from the ones footballers normally need.

The worst danger in Spain he thinks, as they try to relax, will be sun-bathing. Being young healthy men, very conscious of their appearance, they all like to get good sun-tans, but that could be their undoing.

'I want to keep them out of the sun. I want the blood in their muscles, not in their skin. The sun brings too much blood to the surface. They go red and then burn. The sun makes you lethargic. It can also upset your electrolite balance, making you deficient in sodium and salts and you can become dehydrated which leads to exhaustion.'

It is thought by many experts that some of the older players, such as Trevor Brooking, might not survive the heat of the Mediterranean sun, but Dr Edwards has few worries. 'Trevor is very responsible and experienced. They all are. They know how to conserve their energy. They know how to adapt.

In Hungary, the weather was in the 90s right up to the evening of the match, and even then it was about 80. Yet Trevor scored two bloody marvellous goals. If he does that in Spain we won't be doing badly.'

For the World Cup, there will be special drug tests. A Doping Control Doctor will be appointed to whom a list of every tablet which every player receives has to be handed half an hour before each game.

It is therefore necessary not only that the doctor records everything he might give them once they arrive in Spain, but everything they themselves regularly take, perhaps prescribed by their own GP at home. He has no fears that any England player might be silly enough to take something, however apparently harmless, without telling him. Failure to hand in this list can lead to disqualification.

After each match, two players from each team will be chosen at random and submitted to urine tests. This can be agony, all round. Having lost seven to ten pounds in sweat during a match, the last thing most of them can manage is to pass water. The doc has had to sit with one poor England player in the past (whose name he will not reveal) who was unable to make water for three and a half hours.

He is not against late nights, as it is important that the players have relaxation and take their minds off the boredom of hanging around hotels, but he relies on their good sense not to overdo things. Ron Greenwood himself is renowned for treating his players like adults, not little children. 'One can only advise them not to do certain things. At this level, they know enough about the world, and themselves. You want them to perform on the pitch as individuals, so you must treat them as such when they are off it.'

All players, when with their clubs, get a talk from their club doctors each season on the dangers of VD, so Dr Edwards has no need to go into all that. When he was with the Youth Team, he went out of his way to warn them all about temptations, but sees no need with the senior team.

'They know the score. They know the sort of girls who hang around hotels and what can happen.'

One thing about a long trip, and this one could last four weeks is that by being all together, the bad times can seem much worse. There is so little escape. He agrees that the worst seven days in his England family life was after the team's defeat by Switzerland, when they were still abroad, heading for the next match against Hungary in Budapest. Ron Greenwood himself has admitted that every time he met an English supporter in the street, he felt the supporter wanted to physically assault him.

'I'm the only one in the whole coaching party who is not full-time in football. Everyone else has a club to go to at home. So you might not expect me to take things to heart as much, but I do. I try to cheer them all up, set an example, but I feel it deeply as well. The Norway defeat was not as bad. Everyone went home afterwards to their wives and families. They could then comfort us.'

Having checked the water in Spain, inspected the local hospitals, found the nearest orthopaedic surgeon for emergencies, ordered the Mars bars and gone through everything on his normal list, there are of course the minor things that can still go wrong, despite the best precautions.

'The minute I get there, I'll warn them about leaving the hotel and going for a walk. It's a hot day, so what do they do – they feel like an ice cream. That could be highly dangerous. They could have an ice cream from a barrow, one I haven't personally inspected for hygiene. Or they could go into a bar and have a coke. Coke is OK. But while they're not looking, the barman might put ice in it. That could be fatal. You never know where the water's come from.

'I'm looking forward to Spain, but as far as I'm concerned it certainly won't be a holiday . . .'

1982

Enter Harry

A NEW creature has arrived in British football, one whose existence players like Billy Wright could never have imagined. His name is Harry Swales.

You may not have heard of him, unless you happen to be a sports editor of a national newspaper, or work in advertising, television or sponsoring, but what he does should impress you. Harold Swales, MBE, is the agent for England's World Cup football team.

He has kept a dull silhouette and those sports columnists who have had occasional digs at his expense have done so, to Mr Swales's great resentment, without ever having met him. They do not realize, so he says, what a terrific job he does.

He is difficult to meet, especially these days, ever since Paul Mariner, by great good fortune, stuck out a foot to a Trevor Brooking miskick and took England into the World Cup finals in Spain. Until that game against Hungary, all had appeared lost. From that moment, the world and his butler have been after Mr Swales.

For a start, he lives in the village of Collingham, near Wetherby in Yorkshire. Where, you say, asking your personal assistant and your marketing director to get out the gazetteer at once. In the world of agents, where the superstars of the sporting world are controlled from Mayfair or New York by organizations employing hundreds of expensive and beautiful people, Harry Swales is most unusual. He does it all on his own, from his Yorkshire home, with only his wife to help him answer the telephone.

We waited for an hour in the foyer at Grosvenor House Hotel in Park Lane in London where Mr Swales now stays on his regular but fleeting visits to the capital. We watched the mysterious Arabs and their unmysterious daughters, chewing gum through their veils and wearing training shoes. Oh, isn't that Jackie Stewart over there, friend of the Royals? Yes indeed. And that must be Kevin Keegan, wearing an evening suit, our first footballing millionaire.

Mr Swales is also Keegan's agent and he has worked hard to help him achieve household prominence. Keegan was using Harry's hotel room to change in, getting ready for another function. Top footballers spend a lot of time at functions, especially if they are looked after by Mr Swales.

He appeared looking neat and dapper with an RAF moustache which curled across his face, open and to the point, his Yorkshire accent and northern bluntness intact. He is 56 and comes from the village where he still lives. He left school in Leeds at 16 and in 1943 went into the Army, the Royal Horse Artillery, where he served as a driver for six years, in Europe and the Middle East.

He came out in 1947 and became a salesman for Warner Pathé films, working for them for 22 years, ending as assistant sales manager. It was a purely commercial job, selling films to distributors, but through it, he says, he drifted into the world of show business, meeting people in the theatre and then sporting personalities. He also did a lot of charity work for the Variety Club of Great Britain.

About 13 years ago, he decided to set up on his own as a sports agent, having come to know Don Revie and the officials and players of his local club in Yorkshire, Leeds United. Football experts will remember that it was Leeds United who first glimpsed the money to be made out of football—off the pitch as well as on it. Remember all those new shirts, new styles, new gimmicks. I still have a set of number tabs, which you put on your football socks, one of the few ideas not to be commercially successful. It was Harry Swales who did the deal with the Leicestershire firm, Admiral, which is now part of footballing history.

Swales also looked after the players' pool at Leeds. They won the FA Cup in 1972 and he organized their bits and pieces from advertising, photographs, appearances, signed articles and such like. He did such a good job for them that Liverpool asked him to help them; so did Celtic and then Southampton.

It was through Liverpool that he met Keegan. When Keegan moved to Hamburg in 1977, he left Swales virtually in charge of his British commitments. Harry decided this was the time to devote himself full-time to Keegan, which he did. In October 1979, the English players approached him about their pool. Today, he looks after only England and Keegan.

Meeting Keegan was a stroke of luck for him, but the benefit was mutual. So many players, catapulted to success, can easily choose to listen to the wrong advice, swayed by metropolitan manners, expensive suits, knowing ways. Keegan is not just England's only recognized world-class player, he happens to be the smartest, most energetic person to wear an England shirt.

Swales says his role with England is constantly being misunderstood, perhaps wilfully. 'I am not involved *physically* in the lives of the England players, although I get accused of doing so. I would never interrupt their concentration on football. No one in their right mind would want to interfere with the England training schedules. I look after the use of their *image*. Perhaps, after a game is over, they might then be involved physically in some promotion.'

Most football clubs have a pool, if they are at all successful. The FA Cup finalists, for example, will decide to pool all the revenue they can make from their Cup success, dividing it equally between the players, usually from 15 to 18, who are in the first team pool. If they look like doing well, they hand over all the paperwork and negotiations to one person, for a percentage, of course.

The England pool is more complicated. Under Swales, it has developed into an ongoing situation, as of this moment in time. You get a point every time you are named in the England squad. At the end of each year, your points are added up—and under Ron Greenwood almost 30 different players have been called up in the last year—and the spoils are divided according to your points. So even if England had not got to Spain, or even when for months they play no matches, the pool still continues. A commercial firm goes to Swales with an idea, and if they are told yes they pay their money. Oh no, he will not tell us how much. He's not daft.

Trebor, the mints and sweet people, is one of the companies which has official permission to use the England team image, and so has Lipton's. This might mean little more than a photograph of the lads, or it could be personal appearances at company activities.

The biggest current contract is with Courage, the brewers. 'This is really a PR job. We don't endorse their products. We mainly turn up at receptions and meet their clients after an England game is over, of course. About four times a year, they run quiz nights, in a club or factory. Courage invite their clients to put up a quiz team against the England players' quiz team. We never win, though Trevor Francis is exceptionally good, and so is Trevor Brooking.

'We also sign footballs for Courage, which they might give to their local landlords who raffle them, and the proceeds end up for charity. Whenever anyone approaches me for the use of the England team, I put it to a committee of four players—Kevin, Trevor Brooking, Ray Wilkins and Mick Mills. We discuss what would be involved. If we agree it is good for the image of the game, we submit it to the FA for their ratification. So far, everything has been ratified. I am very aware of the responsibility we have. It is important to accept only the right things. We wouldn't accept cigarette firms, for example, or heavy spirits.'

What about Courage? Surely a beer firm is only a stage away from manufacturers of spirits?

'We do *not* advertise beer. We only do internal PR for them. You also forget that Courage is a huge firm. They have hotels and restaurants, as well as everything else. The players have appeared in a campaign for Don't Drink and Drive.

'You either reject or you accept sponsorship in sport. If you accept it, surely it is far better to control it than allow it to become cheap and nasty. We're a sort of policing body. Once we've agreed a contract, we still make sure everything is respectable. Every bit of art work comes to me. If I don't like it, we don't approve it.

'Without us, you would have pirate companies bringing the game into disrepute. As it is, so many people exploit the game without putting anything back. We have done a lot for charity ourselves. We bought six sunshine coaches for the Variety Club. They cost £6,000 each.

'I get upset when people attack what I do. I was asked by the players and the FA to help. People in Britain seem to get pleasure out of knocking anything that is successful. It's a marvellous country, with a marvellous way of life, yet people keep running it down.

'The World Cup is going to be a big occasion, so let's enjoy it, in a responsible manner. It will give a lot of employment to a lot of people. Look at the clothing industry. They've already had a big boost. It could be the Royal Wedding, all over again. Let's be happy about it, rejoice in the success, not be criticising everything all the time.'

Mr Swales received his MBE for his charity work for the Variety Club, not for his services to football. You never know, that might come, now we're going to Spain. His heart must have leapt when he saw that Mariner goal go in. Go on, Harry, admit it.

'No, not for myself. I was pleased for the players. They have to put up with a lot of criticism. And for Ron Greenwood. He is such a gentleman. As for me, I see it as a challenge. I have been indeed very busy since then, but we are willing to discuss projects with anyone. You can get me in Yorkshire. Thank you.'

It's still not absolutely clear how he's managed it. His wife, Audrey, has one suggestion. When you hire Harry Swales, she says, you get Harry Swales, not one of Harry Swales's assistants. Well done, Harry.

1982

Health and Inefficiency

I AM definitely giving up football. And that's final. I'm sitting here once again with an ice pack on my right heel and in half an hour I'll be changing it for my Boots electric heat pad.

I have been going on like this for 15 years, but this really is the end. I can get no sympathy from her downstairs, none at all. Do I tell you all my little worries, she says, when I'm not feeling well, when I have strange pains, no I certainly do not, so please take your rotten foot off the breakfast table.

I just needed some quick advice. Is this a matter for the casualty department of the Royal Free Hospital, they know me so well there I could get a season ticket, or should I struggle on all week and hope to get the swelling down? Come on, please, just tell me what to do? We had breakfast in silence. They have no sympathy in this house.

But my daughter Flora did relent and carried my coffee up to my room and switched on the electric heat pad beside my typewriter and here I sit, contemplating infinity and a very small bruise on my right ankle. Perhaps it's a tendon, not the heel. We do have a consultant in the street, but I think it's urine he's an expert on. Fat lot of use that is.

On Saturday me and old Wrinkly had the most delightful long walk right across the Heath to Golders Hill Park, oh such harmless pleasures, who needs vice or videos. Throughout this little expedition, my knees were trific, no problems, not a twinge. Usually, these days, when I go up any hills, however small, my old cartilage thing plays up, though I'm fine on the flat, thanks for asking.

So yesterday, Sunday, feeling so pleased with myself, I turned out with the lads for our little game. At half-time, I had to limp home, choked as a drain. For some reason, I had got it into my head that the worst I can look forward to, by continuing to play football at the age of 48, I know it's very stupid, don't say anything, the whole street says it to me every week, is that I would weaken my already weak knees. I had never thought I would get a *new* injury at my age. God knows, I have enough old aches to keep me occupied.

My heels, all of them, have been perfect these last 20 years, ask anyone, you never hear Hunt moaning about his heels. Now, my right one feels as if it's a gonner. Must be. I can't stand on the bloody thing. So, finis, exit right, sob sob.

I have so many simple pleasures in life with my dear wife, so why bugger

LITTLE BINKS' FIRST (AND LAST) MATCH.
CROWD:—"GO IT, LITTLE UN! PUSH HIM ORF IT!"

up our leisure life by selfishly courting, nay encouraging, new and awful things to happen to this tired old body. You will never hear me mention playing football again. Goodbye, lads.

What a long pause there. Sorry about that. It wasn't an emotion break, to allow the tears to dry, but I took off the cold pack and switched on the heat. That's better. Give me heat any time.

What it now means, and this is the bitterest bit of all, is that from henceforward, to the last syllabub and the recorded voice of TIM, is that I will have to start eating and drinking sensibly. With playing football all these years, give or take natural breaks for natural breaks, I have convinced myself I can eat anything because I am a person who takes Exercise, therefore I am a fit and healthy person. Must be.

Because of all my injuries in the last nine months, I have put on half a stone. If I became fat in the face or fat in the arms I wouldn't mind, but it's all on the tum, sort of high up, not a beer belly but a BBC coffee belly. That's what done it. Spending two days a week in a BBC studio, I drink endless cups of their lousy coffee.

I have also been getting indigestion, waking up in the night with the most awful stomach pains, oh what a load of moans today, Hunt, I thought this was supposed to be a happy column. A year ago, when I first got this, I was convinced I'd got an ulcer, so the doc gave me some acid tablets, or anti-acid tablets, some stuff called Asilone. They're trific. One chew, and the pain goes. Though these days I have to chew two at least. I think they've gone

mouldy, stuck in my sponge-bag. Or have I got worse? Oh no, don't say that.
I've just got to get better. Playing football does take one's mind off one's
moans.

1982

Souness of Sampdoria

I FIRST met Graeme Souness in 1972 when he was a young player at Tottenham Hotspur. At the time, I was doing a book about the club. He was in the reserves, and never got a first-team match, a rather moody young man, I always thought, sullen, yet aggressive, with enormous chips on his shoulder, convinced the world was against him. He had been brought up in a prefab in Edinburgh and was feeling homesick, unable somehow to fit in. All the other players used to say how good he was, then they'd shake their heads. He appeared to be his own worst enemy, for ever arguing with the management. He ran away once. Then he was suspended. Eventually, they let him go, probably with some relief, for a relatively small sum, just £30,000, to Middlesbrough.

In six years at Middlesbrough, and then seven years at Liverpool, the duckling turned into a swan, if rather a stocky, tough, extremely belligerent swan. Opposition crowds have always enjoyed booing Souness for his aggressive style. But he matured enormously as a footballer, becoming polished and dominant, with an excellent football brain, an inspiring leader who never gives up, becoming captain of the Scottish team.

Off the pitch, he also became known for his style, his clothes, his girl-friends and his social life. He appeared in a TV series, *Boys from the Black-stuff*. Souness is the sort of footballer you could stick in a TV programme. He is known to be intelligent, with great panache, and won't let you down.

When Bob Paisley, as manager, made him captain of Liverpool, he suggested they wouldn't need a ten pence coin any more to toss up with before the match. They'd need a gold card.

He married rather late in life, as footballers go, when he was 27, and as footballers go, his wife is rather unusual. They often go for young hair stylists, from a similar working-class background to their own.

He married Danielle Wilson in July 1980, a divorcée with one daughter. That was unusual for a start. Footballers are terribly conventional. But more surprising is the fact that she comes from a wealthy background. Her father, now retired and living in Majorca, built up a chain of over 100 shops in the Merseyside area. There is a family trust, in which Danielle shares, said to be worth £750,000.

'It worked both ways,' she said. 'No one could say I married Graeme because he was rich and famous. Nor could they say that was why Graeme married me. We married because we were sure of each other.'

Now they are in Genoa, after Graeme's £650,000 move from Liverpool. Danielle recently arrived, as Graeme had gone ahead for pre-season training, along with her eight-year-old daughter Chantelle by her first marriage, and their son, four-year-old Fraser. That day, she'd discovered that another is on the way, due in March. 'I haven't found a gynaecologist yet. They've all been on holiday in August. I'm still waiting for the furniture I've bought.'

The club has put them into a luxury flat, rent free, in a villa in the affluent suburb of Nervi, just outside Genoa. Trevor Francis, the English international player, who has been at the club two years, has the flat next door. That has proved a great advantage.

Trevor Francis, unlike Souness, was a star almost from his first professional game. At 15 he played for Plymouth schoolboys, his home town, and a whole host of top clubs were after him. He chose Birmingham City and was playing in the first team at the age of 16. In 1979, he became Britain's first million pound player when he was transferred to Nottingham Forest for £1,150,000, paying some of it back when he scored the goal which won Forest the European Cup.

In the two years since he moved to Italy, Trevor has adapted well and picked up a lot of Italian. Graeme was going to ask permission for me to watch the next day, but wasn't sure how he would do it. 'The manager doesn't speak English. I don't speak Italian. I'll have to get Trevor to do the translating for me.'

The entrance to the villa and its extensive grounds are through a high gate which is electronically controlled. No stranger can get in, or out, which means that it is perfectly safe for their children and friends to play all day on their bikes, rushing round the villa and the paths. Danielle can therefore get on with her sun bathing. She seemed very fond of sun bathing, like all new arrivals to a hot country.

'When we got married, Graeme said I must be prepared for a move at some time, probably abroad, so it wasn't too much of a surprise. I am pleased for him. It's a short life as a footballer. You should take all the chances you can.

'When I've been in Europe before, I suppose I've always been a tourist, in tourist places, so when you go into a shop, there's always someone who can speak English. I went into a local shop today for sugar, and I asked for it in English, but they didn't understand. I tried to look for it on the shelves, which is what I usually do, but I couldn't see it. So I came out without it.'

'What about a dictionary, wouldn't that have helped?' She shrugged. When things are settled in the flat, then she'll buy a dictionary, not that it will help her to buy some of the minor things she already misses, such as Oxo and Paxo stuffing.

Graeme, meanwhile, had suffered more severe culture shocks in his eight weeks so far. While his wife had been busy with her young family all day, much as she would be in England, doing bits of shopping and talking to other mums, in this case with Helen Francis next door, Graeme had entered a new environment with new sets of rules.

For much of the eight weeks, he had been miles away, up in the mountains, for two long spells, of three weeks and ten days, living a spartan, monastic life. They called this, in Italian, the *Rituro*, and it is like a retreat, keeping the players away from the fleshpots, or even family pleasures, and confined to their remote training camp. The very thought horrifies every British player.

'We were up at seven in the morning and did some early training, then we had breakfast, if you can call it breakfast. Just a cappuccino. Then it was morning training. After lunch, we slept till four, then more training from five till seven. Dinner was from eight to nine, then we had free time from nine to ten. We all had to be in bed by ten. One of the coaches did catch a young player talking to a girl in a bar, *just* talking to her, and he was told off.

'We've had a long talk on what to do about sex generally. Our League matches are on Sundays, so we're allowed to have sex on Monday, Tuesday or Wednesday. But not after that.'

In Britain, training, even pre-season training, normally ends at lunch time every day, then the players go home. And no one would ever dare interfere with their love life.

'The other thing that has amazed me is that Italian players don't drink. After training in England, or after a match, all players have a few beers. They don't here. Perhaps a glass of water, that's all. And they don't "go out" for a drink, the way we do. It's so strange. Italians never think of going out in the evening for a couple of hours drinking in a bar. They only drink when they have a meal, and then of course it's wine.'

As for the football, he has had to get used to different methods. Not better, or worse, just different. 'After all, I played for the best team in Europe for seven years, so I didn't come here expecting the football to be better. I've never hidden the fact that money was the prime motivation.

'I'm having to adjust my play. They play man-for-man here, so before each match there are lots of tactics to understand. In all my seven years with Liverpool, we never worried about the other team. We let them worry about us.'

So far, he had been a success. The Italian League season had yet to get into its stride, but in friendly and in cup matches the team had won their games, with Francis scoring several goals, many supplied by Souness from midfield.

On his arrival 2,000 fans gathered outside the club to greet him. Up in the mountains, he had been amazed one day to find two boys outside their remote training camp, asking if they could take his photograph. He had assumed they were local village lads. 'It turned out they had ridden hundreds of miles from Genoa – on a scooter.'

Football in Italy has an enormous following, yet he had heard little about crowd violence, even though in Genoa there are two rival teams, traditional enemies, Genoa and Sampdoria. 'The worst that has happened to me so far is that when I came out of a restaurant one night, a Genoa fan had put a notice on my windscreen which said "Souness, you are a shit." If that's the worst I'll have to put up with, I'll survive. But one of the lads in the team had his dog poisoned last season by a rival fan.'

It does seem to be the case that in Italy it's the players, and the referees, who get the abuse, rather than the opposing crowd.

'Perhaps in England they should turn their attention on the players, if it would mean less violence. It would be worth the price. The crowds here do behave like human beings, not freaks. But I do miss the singing and chanting from Liverpool. There's none of that. Italians watch a lot of English football on TV and they can't get over all the noises.'

He had also been surprised so far by the lack of perks. In Liverpool, his wife hardly ever had to pay for her groceries or fish, as local people insisted on supplying them free. Most First Division stars in England can manage to get free meals, free furniture, even free cars.

Even more amazing to Graeme, and he knew every home-based Brit player will be appalled at the very thought, Italian newspapers and TV don't pay for interviews. In England, the leading players are paid highly for their ghosted opinions which appear in the popular dailies. They get paid if they do a column for *Roy of the Rovers*.

This had made some of them very greedy, so the British press think, demanding huge amounts just to say I'm over the moon. But the press has only itself to blame for having started the system. (Famous authors or actors never charge for interviews.) In England, most footballers therefore have agents, to do all the negotiations for them.

In Italy, of course, being paid three times as much as in England, it rather makes up for any losses. The previous day Graeme had asked what the fee might be when Italian *Vogue* had contacted him and Trevor to model some pullovers. At home, this could have commanded a rather fat sum.

'I just wanted to see what would happen. I asked the manager to enquire. He said there would be none, and was surprised I'd asked, but I said go on, just see. I've just heard the answer. No fee at all, but we might be able to keep a pullover each. Big deal.'

All the same, he and Trevor think they'll do it, just for the amusement.

That night we all went out for dinner – Graeme Souness, his wife and children, plus Trevor and Helen Francis, their son and friend – to a local restaurant in Nervi, where of course they were treated like the Second Coming.

Over dinner, Trevor explained that there was very little commercialism of footballers in Italy. In a normal year in England, he would expect to attend up to 200 functions, around four a week of some sort, purely in his capacity as a famous footballer. It might be charity appearances, because the club wants you to turn up at a local hospital, or for your own financial advantage, because there's a fee to open a shop or please some sponsor.

'In two years here, I haven't done more than six or seven engagements in a year. The whole system is different.'

He then reassured Graeme that the worst was now over. You don't go to training camps when the League gets into its stride. They play fewer matches in Italy and there are no mid-week games.

'You'll have much more time at home. I see more of Helen than I ever did in England.'

Danielle was very pleased. Back in England, with Liverpool, every season involved so many competitions and travelling to Europe, endless, she hardly saw him during the season.

The women and the children were sitting at the far end of the table. We men were at the other end. Feminism has not yet struck the football world. But being Italy, the wives and children were at least out with the men folk, even though it was quite late at night. In Italy, of course, children are welcomed in restaurants. The men don't go off to the pub on their own.

It was interesting to watch Trevor and his wife Helen speaking Italian so confidently, to waiters, to other people in the restaurant, to fans coming up to them, all with great exuberance and appropriate gestures. I could sense Graeme and Danielle wondering if they would ever get to that stage.

In two years, the Francises have both done well, though not as spectacularly well as their four-year-old son Mathew. He is now bilingual. It had been fascinating to watch him at the villa, playing and shouting with the others children, going from Italian to English, almost without realising. When I first met him, and asked him his name, he replied 'Matteo'.

Trevor and Helen did have a few lessons when they arrived, but gave up quickly. Luckily, they had another footballer, the Irishman Liam Brady and his family, living in the flat the Sounesses now have, to ease them in. (Brady then moved to Milan.)

'I do feel out of it in the dressing-room,' said Graeme, rather wistfully. 'At Liverpool, we used to have such good laughs. Footballers are the same the world over – you get the joker, the moaner, the one who gets picked on. I come in in the morning here and have to sit very quiet while they're chatting away, which is not like me. I feel a bit of a dummy. But och well, I suppose I'll start picking it up soon.'

'He'll have to do it more quickly than me,' said Trevor. 'In his position, he has to shout and be dominant. It's not so necessary for a forward. I know the coach wants him to take control of things. I can sense him getting frustrated when he can't make himself understood. He has to ask me the words at half time or after the match.'

However, he was absolutely confident that Graeme would soon master enough of the language, and then he would love Italy, just as much as he and Helen do. '*Love* Italy? Was it as strong as that?'

'Listen,' said Trevor, 'if someone was to offer me the same money to go back to England now, I wouldn't go. Why should I? I'm happy here'.

'I enjoy the football. It suits me better than England. There's an image in

England that Italian football is defensive. It is, but not so much as it was. It's true that many teams will be happy with a draw and play for that. The Italian League is vitally important and it's taken very seriously, whereas the cup hardly matters.

'When I played for Birmingham City, we struggled almost every season to survive, but we began each game thinking we were going to win. Even if it was Liverpool, we went out convinced we could beat them. Here, if you're playing Juventus or Roma, the big teams, most other teams start off feeling that a draw will be good. And if you do get a 0–0, the players and the crowd go away happy.

'But technically, the Italian players are superior. I would say this is a better league than the English league. Standards have diminished so much in England in the last few years. In England, it is still all blood and guts.

What England has got is the never-say-die spirit. There is such a will to win, with great running power and competitiveness. It means that English league matches can be exciting to watch. Liverpool versus Man. Utd is a great spectacle, as they go at it hammer and tongs. In Italy, the League matches are more like international matches, the sort England now plays, where it's so vital to get a good result and there is a lot of tension.

'Italian football is also not as dirty as British people think. If you go past them, they hate it, but they don't go out seriously to injure you. It's much pettier, shirt pulling, little niggling fouls, spitting at you, but not really nasty. Ask Helen what I used to look like after a normal English game. I'd be a mass of bruises. I can get infuriated here though by the petty fouls. I often think to myself, why don't you give me a good kick and get it over with?

'But on the whole, there is no question in my mind. The football is better. I have recovered the excitement I used to have as a youngster at Birmingham City. I was only 17 when I got in the first team and when we played the big teams, I was knocked out. If it was Man. Utd., I'd ask Charlton or Best for their autographs after the game.

'I now have similar feelings all the time here. Every game there is some player I have always admired or wanted to meet and play against – Maradona, Zico, Rummenigge, Falcao. In England, after 12 years, I knew every English defender I played against, because I'd played them so many times before.

'I consider Platini the world's greatest player at the moment, and it's a thrill for me to play against him. Can you imagine Platini surviving in the hustle of the English First Division? No chance. Yet he's brilliant here.'

Outside football, Trevor and his wife also have no regrets. They have made good friends, fitted in to Italian life, and they even like Italian TV. Both Danielle and Graeme were upset on their arrival to find that when English programmes do appear, they are dubbed into Italian.

'The sport on TV is superb. Every First Division match is shown and every day if there's no soccer on, there's boxing and something else good. They even show Brazilian matches here.

'The weather of course is terrific. Here on the coast, unlike Milan, you're not aware of the winter. There's no snow or ice. You *feel* healthier when the weather is good. It's nice to know it's a wonderful place for my little boy to grow up in. I only miss one thing – the cricket. That's all.'

Graeme nodded his head. In his two months, he had found a few things confusing, but he had no real complaints.

'I *expect* to have complaints. I know that I will have problems some time. It's inevitable, but so far, I have nothing to moan about. The weather, that's been a bit hot for training, that's all.'

What about the other players? Wasn't there some jealousy perhaps, two foreign players swanning in and getting all that attention and much bigger wages than the home-grown players?

'They know if I do well and score goals,' said Trevor, 'they will all gain from it. This whole thing about money and success is so different here. People don't hold it against you that you earn a lot, the way many English people do, especially the press. Here and in America, where I've played a few times, they admire success.'

'Yeh, I've noticed that already,' said Graeme. 'In England, you often get attacked for being a greedy bugger, getting all that money, just to kick a ball around. The British press have built up this image of greedy footballers. But why shouldn't we earn as much as we can?

'In Liverpool, they did try to make me feel embarrassed or ashamed somehow. Earning all that money, while all around there was terrible unemployment and depression. You saw it everywhere you went in Liverpool. I didn't personally feel ashamed about my wage, but I felt uncomfortable.

'In England, I think people don't like you to be successful. It's as if it's a crime to do well.'

Most of the reasons why Graeme moved to Italy are pretty obvious. There's his enormous salary for a start. Then there's all that sun and warm sea for his family to enjoy. But after dinner, as we were walking round the garden of their large villa, he was struck by another, more minor advantage about living in Italy.

It was almost one o'clock in the morning and he had decided to give his dogs some exercise before bed. The night was soft, the stars bright, and we strolled in short sleeves round his garden, in amongst the palm trees and cacti which stretch straight down to the Mediterranean.

'Cuddles,' he suddenly shouted. 'Come here, you little bugger. Where are you? Cuddles!' The Sounesses have an Alsatian called Jock and three Yorkshire terriers called Churchill, Oscar and Cuddles, all of which have gone to Italy with them. Next week, the pony was due to arrive.

In Liverpool, this was always a bit of a problem, taking the dogs round the block before bed. He didn't mind shouting for Jock or Churchill. Even Oscar. But Cuddles. What would his Liverpool neighbours think? Now, in Italy, there was no embarrassment.

141

'It's very hard in England to keep up the macho footballer image, if you have to go around the streets shouting "Cuddles" . . .'

H. DAVIES

1984

Hairy

I'VE BECOME obsessed by hair in sport. Hair, there and everywhere. But most of all right here, where I'm sitting, watching the great and the good on television, giving us the benefit not just of their wit and wisdom but their latest hair styles.

I switched on last Saturday and found myself mesmerised by Dickie Davies's hair. What on earth is *he* attempting to hide? I tried him with the sound off, searching for clues, and he seemed to be talking even more loudly. It would be interesting to see him really worked up about something worthy of his enthusiasm, such as tomorrow's *Sun*. He has a salesman's moustache, saucy sideboards and that dinky bit of grey on top of his carefully brushed head is ever so jaunty. I'd buy a used Page Three girl from him any time.

Brian Moore is about the least hairy of the commentators. I'm always concentrating on his make-up, which often looks as if it's been put on with a trowel. Perhaps this is deliberate, to take our minds off his hair.

Jim Rosenthal has had a lot of bother recently and he still hasn't settled down with himself, or his hair. Same with his smile. He will persist in giving us a full frontal at all the wrong moments.

On the other channel, Harry Carpenter also gets his smiles in the wrong place but whereas Jim Rosenthal lets out an engagingly nervous grin when the studio hand tells him hey up, it's smiling time, there is something a bit menacing about Harry. He speaks quickly but with pointless pauses, and as he comes to the end of his spiel, dramatic pause, quick purse of lips, he lets out a rather wintry, warning flash of teeth. It works in Harry's case. He's been told that the way to be authoritative is to dramatise his diction. Nobody ever worries about his slick of hair.

Then on came Brian Clough. Stand by your beds; no more of this fashion nonsense, lads. He's obviously never been to a barber in his life, far less a hair artiste, and wears his hair exactly as it was when he fell out of bed this morning. Is he deliberately being not affected? I think it's real. He wants us to take him as he is, honest and direct, with no hairs and graces.

Ron Atkinson must spend half his life in his local salon, that's when he's not at the jewellers. Perhaps he and John Bond go together and get trade rates. All those flashing rings are to take your eyes off the back combing, to deflect you from those mysterious bits that grow sideways across his head. John Bond has cocky, very flash hair but Ron, beneath the glitter, is a bit worried. But then, so are they as managers.

I used to feel protective towards Bobby Charlton in his playing days. Steaming down the middle of the park to let go a cracking shot, his hair always got completely out of sync. You could catch him afterwards, the moment of natural delight half ruined by an awful realisation, then a furtive push across his windswept plate. Now in a TV studio, his remaining strands look ever so slick. We don't care, Bobby, I shout. We love you as you are. The golden rule for all those thinning on top is simple: keep it short.

Jimmy Hill has spent a lot of time and money on his beard this season and we must all admire his bravery in letting us at last see the grey bits. Well played, Jim. He now keeps it much shorter these days. Very sensible. Though why does it glisten? Is he watering it to make it grow or is it the heat from the lights or is it caused by that spurious passion he manages to work himself into when giving us a diatribe on the state of the nation and why the rules should be changed or refs be shot at dawn.

I think my all-time favourite hair in football is Frank Worthington's. He's a great stylist, on and off the ball, and over the years he's had as many styles as clubs, usually managing to stay ahead of the herd, although I'm not sure if many other footballers will be rushing to put in the grey streaks. Are they real, Frank? And do you paint on the occasional three-day growth when a big match is coming up and you want to look suitably macho?

You might think it shouldn't matter, all this tonsorial teasing, but it certainly does to players. I remember at Tottenham some of them were near to tears when the away dressing-room didn't have a hair dryer. And if there was no shampoo. Well, sick as parrots, even before the game.

Hair is a vital part of the human display, part of our posture, giving signals about the inner man. Coaches can be very upset by what they consider the wrong hair, but they themselves get the signs wrong, being always behind the times.

In the meantime, I do hope Bryan Robson gives up his dated perm. Poor old England won't ever have a chance in the modern world until he does.

W. EVANS, Tottenham Hotspur.   TOPICAL TIMES

1985

Bobby Robson

BOBBY ROBSON does have a rather nice smile, slow and crinkling, a man of experience who has seen many things, both as a hero and a baddie. He can well remember one of the very bad things that happened to him in life, an event which he realises helped equip him for his job as England manager. He was sacked.

He was aged 34 at the time, back in 1968, and had been a manager in the Football League for only nine months, in control of Fulham, the club he had first played for as a teenager, and whose team had not been doing too well. He was driving home one evening when he noticed a newspaper billboard saying FULHAM TO SACK ROBSON. It was the first intimation he had that his managerial career was about to cease.

Robson went on the dole and for three and a half months he did virtually nothing, hung around the house, took the dog for a walk, became sorry for himself and most of all felt bitter, an emotion he had not experienced before, or since. 'It was an absolutely colossal blow to me, although my wife did her best and was a great support and motivator.'

They had three young boys, two of them at St George's, Weybridge, a local Roman Catholic private school, and the headmaster offered Bobby a part-time job as a football coach, hinting that he might eventually manage to give him enough hours' work at the school to turn it into a proper job.

He thought seriously about leaving football completely and enquired about training to become a PE teacher. But a friend in football offered him some professional scouting work, which kept him in the game, and eventually, hearing that Ipswich was without a manager, he applied and got the job. After a shaky start, Ipswich won the FA Cup in 1978. It's all now football history, part of every schoolboy's mental scrapbook.

Bobby Robson became arguably the most admired manager in English football, creating at Ipswich the most out of the least, building stars by his personality and skills rather than by the glamour of his club or the size of his personal cheque book. In 1982, he was appointed the England manager – to the welcome relief of everyone interested in English football.

I asked him what sort of person he thought he'd be today if he had gone into teaching. He suddenly stopped in his tracks, his Ambassador-for-England smile began to fade and he leaned back in his chair, forehead creased, hand ploughing slowly through his thick, greying hair. Most people who come to his office, the scribes from the back pages, ask simple factual questions, which he does or does not answer, depending on the amount of damage the answers might do. Has Hoddle got a chance, Bobby? Will it be Shilton or Clemence in goal? Do you favour the long ball or short passing? Do you feel sick as a parrot, Bobby, after England's last match? Has Bryan's big toe healed yet, Bobby?

Contemplating his past, thinking hypothetical thoughts about a hypothetical future, are things he is rarely called upon to do. 'Aye,' he began slowly. 'If I'd become a teacher today I would probably be a much nicer person. My wife thinks being a football manager has changed me. Football is full of aggression and competitiveness: you have got to be a winner, your character is forced to change to survive, you become much harder. My family life has suffered, which I regret; I've hardly been at home. I've been unable to do both in life, to be a family man and father as well as manage a football team. It's my fault. I have let the business of football take over my life . . .'

When Bobby Robson married, at the age of 22, his wife Elsie was a nurse. She gave up nursing when they married but as the children grew up she decided to go back to work and retrained to become a primary school teacher.

'When I got the England job I told her that she should give up working as she'd be seeing me again for the first time for 17 years; at Ipswich I had worked round the clock, I was always first in and last out; I really couldn't help it.

'So she gave up the teaching, and you can guess what happened. I'm now working longer hours, partly because our home is still near Ipswich. But the main thing is that this job is far more demanding than I expected – and I still like to be first in and last out. She's now looking for a part-time job, doing supply teaching, but of course times are now difficult in teaching. Aye, it's a hard life for a woman in football . . .'

His own sons are football fans, though they played rugby at school. Paul 26, is an insurance broker. Andrew, 24, is in advertising. Mark, aged 20, is at PE college. They all have saints' names and were brought up as Catholics. It is his wife who is the Catholic, not Bobby: although brought up in a Methodist home, he now considers himself not religious. Nor is he political. Football has been his life.

It all began, as it has begun for so many of our best English players, in the North East. He was brought up in Langley Park in County Durham, the fourth of five boys, son of a miner who missed only one shift in 51 years down the pits. Bobby left school at 15 and became an apprentice electrician down the pit, hoping, as so many millions of boys have done, that one day he would become a footballer. 'Becoming a professional was mysterious. I played for little local teams, but I had no idea how it happened. I worried about how people would *know* about me, how would they *know* I exist?'

Now, from his great height as the England boss, he knows that is never a problem. You keep playing as well as you can, for your local team, *any* local team, and one day you will be spotted. Never fear. There are scouts who have scouts who have scouts.

At 17, he had six real clubs showing interest in him, but to his own amazement he turned down the one around which his boyhood fantasies had revolved: Newcastle United. He had gone the 15 miles every single Saturday with his father to watch them play. 'Even now, when I bleed, I bleed Newcastle's colours. Black and white.'

He chose Fulham, as the man who came to see him seemed the most interested in him, but in London he felt lost and lonely for a long time. He was at first only a part-time professional, on £7 a week, working the rest of the time as an electrician. 'I helped build the Festival Hall.'

After seven years at Fulham, he moved to West Bromwich Albion in 1956 for six years, where he became captain of the team and went on to win 20 England caps, including appearances in the World Cup in 1958. In those days, top players were national heroes, just as they are today, even if far fewer people now go to matches, but they were incredibly badly paid. For most of his playing life, he was on £25 a week. For a win you got £4 extra, and £2 for a draw.

'In my day, you never even thought of playing for money. Winning made no real difference to your pay. Now, in the First Division, the normal bonus is £200. You have to win.' That's over and above the weekly wage. For someone at the top of the First Division today, the going rate is about £1,000 a week or £50,000 a year. For the superstars like goalkeeper Peter Shilton it's probably nearer £100,000.

Bobby Robson says he has never felt any envy, but he saw to it that by the end of his 12 remarkable years at Ipswich he too was being well paid. Many clubs were after him by then, and he was able to dictate handsome terms: his salary is said to be £70,000 for doing the England job.

'I gave up a lot to come here. I was with the nicest club with the nicest board of directors in the country and I was offered a very good contract to stay. But I had always wanted to be the England manager. Who wouldn't?'

He *thought* he knew how it should and could be done. Every fan in the country can pick the best England team. We're all sure *we* know the best players. But; ah ah, it doesn't work that way in practice. For any given match, Bobby Robson is unlikely to have all his *best* players to choose from. The tradition has been that the England manager names a squad of 22 about eight days before a match. This may sound absurd to outsiders, and he thought it far too many, so he decided to name only 18 for one match. Come the day, and five of those had been injured during the intervening eight days and were unable to play. Now he has gone back to 22 – and a lot of finger-crossing.

It has become fashionable to deplore our abysmal record in World Cups and European Nations Cups. The next stage is to jump on and say that therefore English *players* are bad. This is something Bobby Robson won't agree with. If clubs were prepared to release their best players, and let him have their undivided attention well before each match, he knows the England national team would do much better. 'Our clubs win European trophies – that *proves* the talent is there.'

So who is the talent, Bobby, let us know the players you think are world class? Come on, just within these four walls. I promise not to tell any of my friends on the back pages. He hardly paused before he named four English players: Bryan Robson, Peter Shilton, Trevor Francis and Terry Butcher. *Butcher?*

Like a great many fans, at least those outside Ipswich, I have never thought of that hulk as being world class. But no, he insisted that Butcher would get in the national team of any European country. After all, as an Ipswich player, he knew him best of anyone and he had no doubts. Not that personal favouritism *ever* comes into a football manager's mind. They might discover players almost as children, become father figures, shape their whole lives, even grow to love them in their hearts – though they would never admit it – but they can never have favourites. They know that must not be done. Three bad games, and even the apple of your eye has to be cut out and killed.

'Aye, that gap always has to be kept. I make a point of never drinking with my players. You step in. Then you step out.' But he looked wistful as he talked tough.

It is the constant pressure of being the England manager which has surprised him most. 'With a League club, it is hell to lose, but come Tuesday morning, there is another game coming up and you quickly move on. Your pressures anyway are parochial. I had just never realised the national media attention the England manager gets. You get regal treatment everywhere, every door opens. That's another reason why you have to be experienced in life to do this job: being put on a pedestal could go to your head.

'I had imagined I would enjoy the friendly matches. But there are no such things as friendlies with the England team. The pressure is on you for every match. I'd like to experiment and I thought I might be able to throw in four or five new players in any match, but the most I can try is two. You can't toy with players – or with the country. I *must* get results every time.'

1987

Nelson: the Bare Facts

WHATEVER HAPPENED to Sammy Nelson? Oh come on, you can't have forgotten him already. He put the arse into Arsenal. Bum, bum.

Actually, it's a serious question. Stay for the answer and you will be quite surprised when I reveal all.

Sammy Nelson was a member of the Arsenal Double squad of 1971. Lean and tough, keen and eager, if not one of Arsenal's brilliantly gifted players. He would probably have faded by now from non-Arsenal memories were it not for what happened during a match at home against Coventry in April 1979. It's now part of football folklore. Goodness, how we Spurs supporters enjoyed it.

Mr Nelson, for reasons best known to himself, turned to the crowd and dropped his shorts. Ooh. Cheeky. Naturally, his club and the football authorities could not tolerate such disgusting behaviour, bringing the game into disrepute, blah blah. It was not quite a hanging offence, but still terribly serious. He was fined £750 and suspended by the FA for three matches.

Not long afterwards, there was another example of 'mooning', as it's called, by a Wolverhampton player, if I remember correctly. We can't have naked players on our football pitches. He might even have been shot. The punishment seems to have worked, because I can't recall any examples of bare bots recently. Yes, it's true, a lot of fun has gone out of football.

So what of Master Nelson today? Did he join Raymond's Revuebar? Or go to Blackpool and sit in a cage, displaying himself day after day to the punters, like that vicar who got defrocked? Modelling quietly for male magazines, or is he even now delivering strip-o-grams to Spurs Supporters Club parties? All good guesses. All wrong.

Let's first clear up the matter of the bare bum. 'I did drop my shorts,' Mr Nelson told me last week, 'but I was wearing briefs underneath. I wasn't naked. We had earlier given away a goal in the first half, which I'd tried to save on the line, but failed. So when I scored the equalising goal, I just did it. It was to the North Bank, our own fans. The papers made out it was obscene, but it wasn't. I wasn't that type of guy. I was never a hooligan. It was a spontaneous gesture, a bit of fun.'

He did another two years at Arsenal, then moved to Brighton for three years. When that finished, he decided to get out of football completely,

150

having no interest in coaching or managing, or dropping into lower leagues. 'It's sad when people hang on too long.'

At the height of his Arsenal life, he had been earning £40,000-£50,000 a year. He had saved wisely, with a good pension, which meant he could take his time looking for a new job. 'It's very hard to make the transition, to get over that huge gap which suddenly opens up before you when you stop playing. I wanted a completely new challenge, something I could give the same commitment to as in my previous career.'

So he wrote out a CV, listing the eight O-levels he got at school in Belfast, and an FA course he took in leisure management. He sent it to a few PR firms with sporting connections. He managed a few interviews, but nothing came up.

By chance, a friend of a friend passed on his CV to someone at Save & Prosper. He was interviewed and got a job selling insurance and pension schemes. They sent him to London to work, not in Brighton where he still lives with his wife and three children. The theory was that his local fame as a Brighton player would not help him. After all, who would take financial advice from a mere ex-footballer?

Now he has been promoted to an underwriter. This is not quite on the scale of the Lloyd's version, but it means he can underwrite up to £75,000 on his own behalf, without having to go to his superiors. He greatly enjoys the work. 'I believe in what I'm doing. I know from my own experience that pension planning is a good thing.'

Moral: always start at the bottom.

PS: For Arsenal fans, four of the Double team are still in football: Graham, Rice, McLintock in England, Armstrong in Kuwait. One is in TV: Bob Wilson. McNab was last heard of in real estate in California, Storey in the rag trade, Sammels in a driving school, Charlie George in a garage. Ray Kennedy is suffering from Parkinson's disease.

1988

The Man in Black

I HAD quite a few surprises when I observed my first private gathering of soccer referees. We're so used to them in their black shorts and black shirts. Very busy, rather bossy. No one expects them to sleep in their kit, or go out socialising with naked knees, but they did look strange in their best long trousers, neat blazers, county badges, shiny faces, shiny short hair – every bit as grown-up as school prefects.

It was the 'Eve of the Cup Final Rally' at a London hotel, a posh do attended by 450 referees last May to honour the chosen ones, the lucky referee and linesmen about to take charge at Wembley the next day.

It's an annual occasion, for members only, and I was fortunate to be there, privy to their private rites. It is a chance for the Wembley ref to mix with his own kind, well away from any possible contamination by fans or footballers.

There was an awfully clean cabaret, and a girl singer got all the refs to sing along, and there were stalls selling personal requisites, such as the Chromium-Plated Acme Thunderer Whistle, only £1.60, or plastic finger-whistles, 75p.

The evening finished with a touching ceremony in which the Wembley ref and his officials got presented with something or other. Then came the bit that I'll never forget.

A huge queue started forming, with hundreds of blazered refs standing patiently in line, clutching their Wembley programmes. I couldn't understand it at first. Then I realised. They were waiting to get autographs of the Wembley ref and linesmen. I had never imagined that refs would be groupies.

There are 25,000 qualified referees in the four home counties, so running the Cup final is like winning the Nobel Prize. All the Sunday-afternoon park refs fantasise that it could be them.

Britain gave soccer to the world, but in 1863, when the first FA rules were written, referees were not mentioned. Players were meant to know the rules and stick by them. The referee officially appeared in 1881, when the FA Challenge Cup began, but he was off the pitch, checking the time, keeping the score. He didn't arrive on the pitch until 1891, complete with whistle.

They have proper training today, with beginners' classes held around the country. It's then a long slog up to Grade One status and the Football League, which normally takes ten years. You'd be quicker training as an architect or doctor, and better off. But they do it for the love of the game.

Find the Referee.

what an ass—
—pect

⋆ ⋆ ⋆

Here we are in room C in the basement of Birkbeck College in the University of London. It's Monday evening, the nights are drawing in, but nine likely lads have been drawn off the street, away from the telly, to do some studying. Half, by chance, are Greek Cypriots. One is Asian. There are no blacks and no women. They have six weeks of study ahead of them, after which they will have an exam, a practical and an oral.

Their teacher, Stan Nathan, is taking them through some very complicated

153

rules, and some sophisticated definitions of the English language. What do we mean by 'accidental'? How do we decide an action is 'intentional'? It could well be an OU philosophy class.

From time to time, if they don't understand the deeper meaning, he gives them a cuff, or a few well chosen words of admonition. 'You're just thick. We've got a right idiot here tonight.'

At the end of this particular evening he sets them some homework. 'Right, I want you to write down this quotation: "Referee, that was a fucking awful decision." Now, would you send this player off or caution him?'

There are classes like these going on in places throughout the country. Over 4,000 new recruits come forward every season, hoping to qualify as Grade Three referees. They will be able to wear their county badge on their ducky black shirts and referee Sunday-morning matches between local park teams. For this, they will get between £8 and £10 a match. And a great deal of abuse.

The vast majority, some 15,000, stay as Grade Three refs for ever. Advancing to Grade Two and Grade One is done by putting in the years, and applying to be endlessly assessed. At the top of the tree, there are presently just 94 refs who turn out for the Football League, and for that they can get £100 a match.

They are not little Hitlers, as many spectators allege, nor on an ego trip, as players often think. They're simple blokes. They were not good enough as players to get very far, and in their real day-jobs the chances are that they will not be high flyers either. Anyway, you couldn't do both. A top ref does it almost full time these days, with the travel and training, so he needs a very considerate employer.

They like it that way. They know that the top players get £1,000 a week, but they're not jealous. They say being full time and getting a proper wage would not make them better refs. They enjoy their amateurish status, part of the football industry, yet not really in it, relying on voluntary work and voluntary workers up and down the country to organise all the nation's referees, their meetings, their magazines.

But they have problems. While 4,000 are currently starting, there are 4,000 currently packing it in. It's not just the abuse, but the violence, being punched and attacked, during and after matches. In 1988 there were 370 physical assaults on referees. They put most of the blame on society, but they would, wouldn't they? In this day and age, so they argue, we do not have respect for authority, any authority, least of all those armed only with a little whistle and a notebook. In the Football League, they can hurt, and players don't like being suspended. But in the park, it's fairly meaningless, sending off a bloke. How can you check he's not playing next week, among 500,000 Sunday-morning players?

There are only two black refs on the Football League list (one Asian and one Fijian, to be precise), a disgrace really, when you think that the average club these days can have a third of the team made up of black players. The Referees' Association wants them to apply, but they don't. As for women, there is none so far, though there are no rules against them. The highest woman ref I could find was Jill Morgan who, to date, has done only Vauxhall Opel League matches. (That's a level below the Fourth Division.)

Nonetheless, our refs are very proud of what they do. In fact, they boast that the British referee is the best in the world. That's what Peter Willis maintains, president of the Referees' Association. His proof is the number of times our top refs get invited abroad to referee foreign matches.

It's an interesting thought. While our native football gets worse in relation to the rest of the world, our refs get better. Perhaps because of it. Think of all they have to control – those rotten British matches, played at full, bad-tempered pelt. Survive them, and you can survive anything.

1989

Souness of Rangers

OUTSIDE IN the street are young girls, would-be groupies, waiting for autographs. Inside the marble entrance hall, beside the marble pillars, are deprived families, waiting to be blessed. Cripples in wheelchairs, babies in arms, all dressed in blue. It could be Lourdes, or an early Beatles concert, innocent people, hoping for magic.

The uniformed commissioner is being kind, talking to the faithful, saying not long now, they'll just be finishing in the bath. Behind him, in the main doorway, a security guard stands silent. To keep out the groupies? Protect the handicapped?

A secretary emerges and hands a blue envelope to a boy in a wheel chair. His mother opens it for him. A little pennant, some Rangers souvenirs. Och, isn't that nice, Willie?

At last, the first Hero appears – Trevor Steven, an Englishman, but a hero nonetheless to all true Gers supporters. Now it's Big Terry Butcher, club captain. Then a black man, Mark Walters, followed by Ally McCoist, and then oh joy, it's Mo Johnston. Each is a model gentleman. Not just the striped shirt, impeccable creases, expensive hair, but the natural charm.

'How you doing, pal?' each one speaks in turn to the crippled boy, shaking his hand, bending down to chat as the mother fusses, getting her camera ready. 'Who's your favourite player then?'

'I have to say you are,' mumbles Willie. Every player laughs, almost the same laugh, then gets up, shakes hands, and they shamble like sailors across the marble floor. Footballers are not good walkers.

At the main door, the Security Man awaits just one player. He falls in behind Mo Johnston. There were threats on his life when as a Catholic he signed for Rangers. His safety is still being permanently maintained.

Another morning of training is over. The players are free, but most fans are hanging on. Will they get to see the best known face of all, Graeme Souness, Britain's richest footballing man?

He arrived three years ago from Italy on a salary of £200,000, which makes him our second-best paid manager. Terry Venables of Spurs is thought to get more, having come from Barcelona. But Mr Souness is unique in British football. He is also a director. He paid £600,000 for ten per cent of the shares, currently worth £4 million.

The fans are not concerned with such vulgar monetary thoughts. They want to see this 36-year-old man who has put Rangers at the top again in Scotland, after ten poor years, and turned it into the best club in Britain.

He looks stern when he eventually appears, with that cold stare, the severe moustache. Their faces had lit up at the very sight of Mo and Ally, but should they perhaps not stand to attention for Mr Souness. Put a foot or a word wrong and might he not kick, just as he did opponents in the old days? He was hardly popular as a player. Should they love him as a manager?

He does his bit, hello pal, smiles and poses for the happy snap, but they keep their distance. Not many people know what to make of Graeme Souness, or how to handle him . . .

The manager's office at Ibrox is about the size of the Albert Hall, plush with blue leather and blue soft furnishings. He was having his lunch, fruit salad and tea. 'You don't have to have this. Order anything.' Staff hovered, then were dismissed. Beside him was Walter Smith, the assistant manager, an appointment made for him in 1986, when he took over as manager, but one which has turned out successful.

'I didn't plan to leave Sampdoria. The President of the club, one of the most honest Presidents in Italy, had recently called me in, asked if I was happy. When I said I was, he sold the player who might have been the rival for my position. I had another year on my contract. I was very happy. Then out of the blue, the Rangers offer came. An offer I could not refuse.'

Oh come on, surely you must have set it up? 'About three months earlier, I had been back to Scotland for Jock Stein's funeral. In a TV interview, someone had asked if I ever thought of coming back to Scotland, and I said no, not really. Only one job would tempt me back – managing Rangers. Then I got on the plane to Italy and forgot all about it. There had been no calculation. It was an off-the-cuff remark.'

The hardest thing was playing *and* managing. 'I've always prided myself on physical fitness, that's part of my game, but being player manager was difficult, with driving thousands of miles. It was also hard to mix with the players, to carry on the sort of life I'd led for the last ten years. I still train with them, as I did this morning, and they take the piss out of me, but I've stopped playing. This is my first season purely as manager. I have a better relationship with them now.'

Next hardest job, and one he still does not relish, is dealing with the press. 'Rangers command more media attention than any other club in Britain. Oh, miles more than Liverpool. They don't have national papers on their doorstep twice a day. We live in the limelight here. The Scottish papers know that something about Rangers on the back page or even better the front page will sell copies. It's just like Italy. Permanent aggravation. I remember when Joe Fagan was being asked to take over at Liverpool. He said he would, as long as someone else dealt with the press. No manager likes that part.

'They expect you to comment straight after a match, when you're all hyped up. Someone throws a controversial question at you, so you lash out. Great for the press, but you regret it later. For an ex-player, it's very hard to adjust. But we always talk to the press here, after every match. If we lose, it's always me. If we win, then Walter might do it.'

Why the difference? 'If I didn't turn up after a defeat, it would be used against me.'

There was a third problem he worried about when he took over. How would he sack someone? 'It did bother me a lot, until the first time. It turned out easy. No problem, if you feel it's the best thing for the club. I've now done it, well, many a time.' He refused figures, for players or staff, but smiled, ruefully. In three years, there has been a massive turnover, of people arriving and departing, from young hopefuls who never made the team, to star internationals. Recently, the Chief Executive departed, after what was described as a power struggle with the Manager.

The 'foreign' stars were forced upon him, as the Scottish clubs would not sell to Rangers, so he had to raid abroad, in England and Europe, regardless of colour, race or creed.

'I knew some people would be upset when I signed Mo Johnston. It didn't worry me. I'm the custodian of this chair and I do what's best for this club. I now have one Jewish player, as well as a Catholic, but that hasn't had such publicity. I don't give a monkey's what they are. Are they good enough? Will they do it consistently? That's what matters.'

So far, he has spent almost £12 million. 'I reckoned that with success, we would get bigger gates to pay for it all.' When he arrived, the gates were averaging 18,000. Last season, it was 40,000, the biggest in Britain. The stadium is now practically all-seated. While most football club fanzines tear their club and players apart, the Rangers fan mag seems to have only one complaint – they can't get tickets. 'We've just spent £3 million to make it the best stadium in the country. Now we're going to spend £13 million on a new tier to hold 50,000, all-seated, and make it the best in the world.'

In his own career, he was not always popular, but it never worried him. 'At school I was the same. You say that at Spurs I had chips on my shoulder, so what's wrong with that? It may be good in life to think the world's against you. You fight harder. I never cared what the public thought, just people like Jock Stein, or my own family.'

He once broke the jaw of a Rumanian, unseen by the referee. Not exactly a good example for younger players?

'That was stupid and I regret it, though it was retaliation. I cared so much that I did do daft things in the heat of the moment. But I think it helps, not hinders, me as a manager. I can understand people like me.'

There have been rumours that he might swap places with Kenny Dalglish, manager of Liverpool, which he dismisses as rubbish. 'I already have the best job in Britain. Why should I move? This team is in its formative years. I've got a long way to go. I'd like Rangers to be the top team in Scotland, every year, and be top in Europe. That would be success. And if I'm not doing it, and I think another manager could do better, then I'd leave. I love this club, and want it to be successful.

'The quality of life in Scotland is the best in the UK. There are no racial problems, no traffic jams. Every time I go to London all I see is poverty.'

He paused. Nine months ago, his wife left him, taking their children, disappearing to her father's £4 million Spanish home, followed by the hacks, desperate for the full story. There appears to have been no other person, on either side. His wife could no longer put up with a back seat, stuck at home, while her husband devoted his life 100% to football. He was left with their brand new £1 million mansion near Edinburgh, complete with swimming pool, stables, tennis court. It was built with seclusion and security in mind, and has come in handy. Mo Johnston is at present living there. Graeme is in a rented flat in Edinburgh, near his father's home.

'I don't really want to talk about it. I'm not the first football manager to whom it's happened. You can be tremendously well paid in football, but there are sacrifices. It's very time consuming. I did spend too much time away from my home.'

The divorce is now going through, amicably, if expensively. His wife has returned to London and he sees the three children regularly. Chantelle, 14, and Fraser, eight, are at boarding school. Jordan is aged four. 'They do matter to me more than anything else.'

That afternoon, being Friday, he took an hour off, his first break from football all week. We went to the Motor Show in Glasgow. He tried out a £100,000 Mercedes, although his present one has done only 2,000 miles, and tried to avoid any Celtic fans. We saw one, dressed all in green, so he walked behind a pillar. No need to put up with abuse on an afternoon off. But for Rangers fans he smiled, did autographs, posed quickly for snaps.

He also takes a prettier picture these days. Just examine that nose. Five times he had it broken in a playing career. After his final match last May, in the Cup final against Celtic, he decided on a nose job, to have the nasty bumps straightened. 'It has helped my sinus, but that wasn't the real reason. I admit it. It was 99% vanity.'

Have you got a girlfriend, then, hmm? He shook his head.

Will you marry again? 'That's the furthest thing right now from my mind. Come on, I must get back to Ibrox. . . .

1989

Wembley Stamp of Approval

I'M GOING to Wembley tomorrow to see England against Italy, along with my son and heir. We are in block H, row 21, in the cheapo £15 seats. Plus £2 booking fee. What a cheek.

It's a treat for him as he's fresh from tefling in Turin. Oh come on, Teaching English as a Foreign Language. I bet you wish you were coming with us, if only to enjoy our conversation. It so happens that I'm a world expert on Wembley. Ask me anything. While my dear son is a planet pundit on Italian football. Perfect combination.

Right, Wembley. It started through philately, one of my many collections. I did Penny Blacks first then I decided to specialise in Wembley. As you well know, the first commemorative stamps in the UK came out in 1924 to celebrate the Empire Exhibition at Wembley.

They built the Wembley stadium as the focal point of the Exhibition and the 1923 Cup final was held there. The stadium was considered a miracle of ferro concrete, a wonder of the world in 1923, doing for concrete what the Crystal Palace did for glass, some 70 years earlier. To test it out, before the 100,000 fans were let in, a whole battalion of soldiers marked time in the stands.

The Empire Exhibition was a huge success with the public, but it went bust and most of the buildings were sold off. The Palestine Pavilion became a Glasgow laundry. The East African Building became a jam factory. Several cafés were rebuilt as Bournemouth and Boscombe FC's grandstand. Only the stadium remains today.

It looked white in those days, not grubby as it is today, but I won't have a word against it. I love the shape, the towers, the elegant brutality of it all. It's still the best known football stadium in the world. Stuff the San Siro.

OK, on your marks for the Italian team. Are you listening, Bobby. Jake says they only have one exceptional player, Baresi. He's not big but he'll blot Lineker out of the game, now that Lineker has lost his speed. Then they have two exciting players, Donadoni and Maldini. Zenga is a good goalie, but does even better as a TV personality. Did you know he has his own show? He's the working girl's Wogan.

Most attention will probably be on Vialli of Sampdoria, for whom both Milan and Juventus are said to be willing to pay £9 million, repeat nine

160

World Cup 1986: some pretty artistic stamps, all unused

million. That's about nine Linekers. Vialli has a good work rate, unusual in Italy, but he misses a lot of goals and can be psyched out of a match. So get someone to hassle him, Bob.

Serena of Inter is skilful and scores a lot of goals in the Italian League, but he relies on the German players to provide them. They won't be playing tomorrow.

'The way England can beat Italy is to play like Arsenal. That's the way I hate football being played, but it will work. Up in the air, and grind them down. If that fails, send for Bull. Don't bring on Waddle. They'd just laugh at his dummies.'

But come on, Jake, we haven't got the technique, have we, that's what all our clever clog football commentators tell us.

'People confuse technique with skill. Barnes and Beardsley are "natural" players, just as skilful as anyone in the Italian team. Skill is not learnt. What the Italians have learnt is ball technique, so they look more comfortable. What the English learn is physical stamina and team play. That's how we've got to play to beat them.'

But the Italians have learnt that as well, so it seems to me. Isn't 'pressing' now the most popular English word in the Italian language? I've been reading your Eyetie sports pages. 'Sempre pressing', that's how they describe the Milan style. And I think you're dead wrong about Waddle. I'd have him in my team.

'No, tackle is the most used English word on their sports pages. They don't have an Italian word for it.'

Well, what do you know. For example. I bet you were unaware that in 1940, thousands of evacuees from Dunkirk slept here, in Wembley Stadium, on their first night back in Blighty.

Look, just sharrup, eh. The match is about to start . . .

162

1989

Why I Hate Spurs

I AM faced with the most awful moral dilemma. I am not sure if my conscience will allow the obvious decision. How could I ever face my friends? My Saturdays would never be the same again.

I am agonising as a football fan. They are the only people in football concerned with moral or philosophical problems. Players are mercenaries, they don't give a damn, they have no faith, no loyalty, they will go anywhere, do anything, if the money's right. Look at Mo Johnston. In his confessional, they would have to do extra time.

Look at managers. Swear it's for ever, swear they really care, swear they're doing it for the community, but we all know that, like players, half of them don't know what town they're in. Just feel the wage packet.

And directors. Do they care? Do they heck. That bloke who tried to buy Manchester United. Didn't he also try to buy Bolton? Call him a true supporter. They are less faithless than players or managers, but only because they have less opportunity to move around.

You can go anywhere, as a fan. No one is paying you. You have signed nothing. You have total free will. Yet in your bones, you know you have no choice. You can't change colours. For better or for worse. *Your team* is your team. Till death do you part.

It's a very strange relationship, which doesn't happen in the real world, outside Saturday afternoons. People who work for Sainsbury's can be head-hunted, just as players or managers in football. But the customers of Sainsbury's also move around. They feel no compunction about going for the better attraction, the bigger bargain. Why is it different in football? We're all paying consumers. We all have free choice. Ah, but we don't. We have brainwashed ourselves.

Most football fans, in the first place, get 'chosen', rather than choosing a club. It's their home town team. Their family have always supported it. So it goes.

In 1959, when I first came to London, I had no local allegiances. I looked at the map of north London and could have chosen either Spurs or Arsenal. Both seemed handy, but Spurs were doing better, played more attractively, so they became My Team.

Over 30 years I have given them total devotion. I hate Arsenal. Obvious,

163

innit. I'm sick as a frog when Spurs lose and gutted when Arsenal win. I tell people we have two excellent teams in north London. Spurs and Spurs reserves. Ha ha. When someone says they're an Arsenal fan I say, quick as a flash, oh you don't follow football then.

OK, so Arsenal have done better in recent years. OK, so Arsenal have actually won things. I might even admit, forced against the wall, they have quite a good team at present. So what? Come on, you Lillywhites. There is no going back. I made my bed, now support it.

But should I? Spurs don't care about me, why should I care about them? Ah, but it's not a matter of logic. We're into blind faith here. A Spurs supporter supports Spurs. End of story. End of life.

I've only got one life. Why should I put up with misery? Why should I not be promiscuous and move around with my favours?

I usually have a cold shower when these disgusting thoughts enter my head, but in the last year certain things have dawned on me:

I hate the Spurs programme. Yuck. Glossy pix, but appalling prose, aimed at idiots. No wonder football fanzines have taken off. There's no competition. I feel cheated of £1 every time I buy it.

I hate the Spurs merchandising. Football appears to have taken a back seat to commerce. In the last League programme, against Chelsea, there were eight pages devoted to selling Spurs kit. Hurry, hurry for a New Spurs Dressing Room T-shirt, only £8.99, or a New Spurs Suit Carrier, £19.95. I feel sorry for the players. Having to pose like dickheads, wearing all this junk. And the parents whose kids want to buy the stuff.

I hate the new board. The old directors were pathetic, totally out of touch, but the new board seem only in touch with the sponsors.

I hate the executive boxes. If I see another list of their names I'll scream. We're supposed to be grateful to these banks, property companies, hotel groups, international businesses for lashing out their shareholders' dosh.

I hate the ticket office. Every season, they seem to muck up my tickets, or they get nicked in the post. Order by phone and credit card and they charge you £1 extra. Bloody cheek. The seat tickets anyway are ridiculously expensive.

I hate the new press box. It was good in the old days, but now it's so low you can only follow half the match. They obviously preferred to flog off the better positions.

I hate Holsten. This is the sponsor. Yes, I know all clubs have them, but it still upsets me to see their name on the breast of every player. I am a shareholder, and I understand the commercial reasons, but it's the smell which sickens me, the kowtowing for money.

I hate getting to Spurs. It now takes me 45 minutes, through horrible high streets which are always chocka every Saturday afternoon.

I hate the present team. There, I said it. You'll wonder why I never said it first. But all the trivial reasons do matter, and annoy me every week. And it's true that if the team were brilliant, I would forget all the other complaints.

"TURF" CIGARETTES

W. E. NICHOLSON
TOTTENHAM H.
50   FOOTBALLERS   N⁰ 42

The last time they went down, I did support them, even going to away matches, and there was a great community feeling, as if they somehow did not deserve it. Now, having spent £8 million, who will feel sorry for them? Do I hate Venables? Hard to, when he's obviously such a nice bloke, but his days must be numbered.

So what have I done? Don't repeat this, but for the last year I've found myself going to Arsenal when Spurs have been away. What a traitor. What a turncoat. No, hold on. I have been going purely to see them get stuffed.

I can get to Arsenal in 20 minutes through back doubles, and the parking is better. Their programme is just as boring and they now have executive boxes, but they seem to have put them up with far less fuss and inconvenience.

Could I become a Born Again Arsenal supporter? Blank out the past, forget these 30 years and start again? That would be the logical solution, feeling as I do. It's what my wife recommends. It's only football, she says. People change nationalities, change religions, change wives. Why upset yourself so?

I think it would take hypnotism to make me sit there and honestly shout for Arsenal. I love Spurs. Always will do. I will support no other. That's the way it goes. Tra la. But as with so many forms of Love, Hatred is not so very far away. I remember talking to Morris Keston, a lifelong loony Spurs fan. He never watched the last 15 minutes of any game. It was all too unbearable. Even when they were winning, he knew it might well end in tears. His Love for Spurs was Agony.

Once you're part of a football family, then Love is taken for granted. You are allowed to criticise, as in any Family, which is something the club's programme has never understood. Naturally, if an outsider dares to criticise, then that's out of order. But amongst ourselves, we are allowed to boo, hiss, mock, jeer and scream inwardly when Gazza retaliates like an idiot.

In calm moments, I know only too well that nothing I can think, or the most abusive shout on the terraces, or the nastiest shit-stirrer write in *The Spur*, will ever equal the pain and despair which the players themselves suffer. They know and feel the agony better than we do, and have to live with it, seven days a week. We can go home on a Saturday, kick the tele, switch on the wife, and settle down with a Holsten Pils, be sick, and get it over with for another week. They can't escape.

The manager knows the worst – AND LONG BEFORE WE DO. He is watching those dummies he bought day after day. He sees loss of form before we do. He knows of injuries we'll never hear about. He knows the idiots who will never improve. The ones with domestic daftness buggering up their lives. The ones on drink or dope. The ones who can't be told. The ones too thick to learn. The cowards and cheats. I should think in any one month he feels more Hatred for his players that we do in a lifetime. And also Love.

So, should we have more pity on the poor suckers? Do they not bleed when we carp and criticise? Of course they do. And they hate us for hating them, thinking as Loyal Supporters our duty is to offer Blind, Unswerving Support. Hard cheddar.

We fans do not pay our hard-earned money to be kind, to contemplate politely in the calm moments, to consider carefully the feelings of the players and the manager. They have chosen to be up there. No one forced them, and they get quite well rewarded. They must be prepared to be shot at, shat on, like politicians, rock stars, writers. Dear God, you should see the horrible book reviews I've had over the years.

The trouble is, I've waited almost 30 years now for another team capable of taking the First Division. Bloody hell, it's Spurs, not Carlisle United, I'm twittering on about, one of the all-time great clubs, upon whom enormous North London love and several fortunes have been spent. As it is, I have to face facts. I know, as we all well know, that they have neither enough truly talented individuals nor shaped what they have got into a formidable, fighting unit.

But, hope springs, love will last, hatreds will come and go, and Spurs will travel on. As we all will, following them into the Nineties. Good luck, and thanks. For the Memories, if little else.

CHURCHMAN'S CIGARETTES

W. HALL (TOTTENHAM HOTSPUR)

1990

Aching for Past Glories

I WATCHED my team last weekend. I felt so sad, so wistful, so mournful, that I had to hurry on, lest a tear might fall. No, not Tottenham Hotspur. Though goodness knows, they would make strong hooligans weep. Nor even Carlisle United. And they do worry me a little at present, poised for so long to climb out of the Fourth, yet will they keep their grip?

I'm thinking about Dartmouth Park United. No need to check them on your pools. And you won't find them in Rothmans. But they are a real team, registered with the local council, and they play each Sunday morning on Hampstead Heath, London, England, Europe, the Universe.

They happen to be *my* team. For the simple reason that I begat them. Not many of us, as we struggle through this mortal whatsit, can boast that we will bequeath to posterity a football team.

It all began over 20 years ago. I was in my early thirties, two young kids, Miele washing machine, stripped pine wife, our own tortoise, the usual stuff. I'd given up competitive football, playing in local leagues, travelling away every second Saturday. Well, you can't, can you, not with domestic duties to attend to. Then one day, on the Heath, I got talking to another dad, dragging a pushchair while kicking a ball, just as I was doing, and I said, wouldn't it be good if we had a dads' team, just for the likes of us. Little did we know, etc. that life would never be the same again.

Gosh, what pleasure I had all those years. It was the highlight of my weekend. Such arguments we had over who was picking the two sides. Such troubles I had getting subs out of people to pay for the pitch. Such scenes during the game, as we argued over fouls, and fouled over arguments.

I got rid of such stress and tension, just by taking part, although I was hardly aware of this at the time. It's only now, since I've retired, that I see how bad tempered I have become. And I know, without any quack telling me, that the various jaw aches and ear aches and leg aches I now suffer from are due to not playing football. Bound to be. They only started after I finished.

It was the old body that went, not the psyche. I recovered from one cartilage operation, and made a triumphal return. *Hurrah, Hunt is back.* I can hear the cheers across Parliament Hill even now. Then I had a second cartilage. This never properly healed. Nonetheless, I struggled on. On

BERT BLISS

TOTTENHAM HOTSPURS

T. CLAY

TOTTENHAM HOTSPURS

J. DIMMOCK

TOTTENHAM HOTSPURS

W. JAQUES

TOTTENHAM HOTSPURS

Mondays I would often be unable to walk, unable to drive, ruining our family life, little use to anyone for most of the week, covering myself in heat pads, shoving on patent gunge, just to be ready for Sunday. When I would get injured, once again.

Don't say it. That was really stupid. I probably knocked years off my life, by carrying on too long. But I got to 50, which was my ambition, and finally hung up my socks, threw out the heat pads, binned the bottles of embrocation.

The team goes on, to further strengths. My son Jake, a baby when we began, is now a stalwart. There are some founding fathers still playing, including one bloke of 60. I hate him, I really do.

Real footballers rarely watch football. On a Saturday off, they can't bear it. I felt the same, but it was very hard that first year. I forced myself to street markets on Sunday morning, collectors' fairs, buying junk for my various dopey collections, just to take my mind off my misery. I now have a pattern of sorts, and created a new shape to the weekend. Life goes on, such as it is.

Last Sunday, when I was wandering back across the Heath from Camden Lock, my mind must have been elsewhere. I heard these oaths, these awful shouts, people squaring up to thump each other. My friends, my band of brothers, engaged in mortal whatsit. I pulled my cap down and ran. I was running away from my old life, from memories too sad to remember.

1990

Football in the Cameroon

I WENT to a football match last week. Normally it takes me half an hour's drive and with my Spurs Member's card it costs me £6 to get in. No sweat.

This match took me ten days. I covered almost 10,000 miles, travelling there and back. Together, me and Geoff, the photographer, spent almost £5,000 of *You* magazine's money. That's including fares, hotels, presents, pills and assorted bribes.

As for the sweat, bloody hell. Not just the stuff that pours off you but the panics in the mind. At various times I was convinced I was a goner with malaria, that we would end up in jail or perish in the jungle.

All for a piddling football match? Well, why not, if you seriously consider yourself a football fan? We know where our priorities lie. Football is not just a matter of life and death. It's much more important than that, as the Blessed Shankly once said.

Just think of what is going to happen on 8 June 1990. Billions and billions round the globe will be tuned in to the first match in this year's World Cup. It will feature Argentina, the holders, and their world stars such as Maradona. Their opponents will be Cameroon. Pardon? What did you say? Who are they when they're at home?

Precisely. That was our quest. To see football, at home, in the Cameroon. Venture where none of our soccer hacks has been before. Where no pink 'uns are seen. Where no millionaire footballers exist. Where football is pure and innocent. By looking at a different form of football, compared with our home-grown variety, might we not see a different sort of life?

The heat hit us so hard when we got off the plane at Douala that I could hardly breathe. It was like being stripped, mugged then shoved in a Turkish bath, all in one blow. Cameroon is in the armpit of Africa. Very appropriate, hot and sweaty and very hairy. Between Nigeria and Equatorial Guinea, just three degrees above the Equator.

From Douala, we got a local plane, some 200 miles inland, where it's higher and not quite as equatorial, to the capital Yaoundé. Again another new name, yet with a population of 750,000. How ignorant we are in Britain. Okay, I am.

It was late at night when we crawled into our hotel, on a hill just outside the city, the Sofitel Mon Febe, said to be the best in the whole country. We dragged ourselves to the bar, draining our last bit of energy. The whole hotel seemed totally empty, yet sitting around the lounge area were about 20 sensational looking girls, beautifully dressed, marvellous posture and bearing. Must be some sort of dance troupe, I thought.

As we supped, one of the girls came up, flung herself round Geoff's head and then began feeling his body. All over. Then another stunner sat down beside me and asked for my room number. She'd like to visit me, privately. We fled. Didn't even make our excuses.

I spent the first three hours on the phone next morning, ringing Fecafoot, the Cameroonian FA, then various Government departments, very slowly and bad temperedly getting nowhere. There are few phones anyway in Cameroon. By midday, I felt I had tried every one in the whole country. My bedroom phone was wonky and every number had to be dialled three times. So it goes.

The first day on a story in a strange country is always deeply depressing. No one knows you, no one cares. Afterwards, I always come home feeling sorry for every foreign correspondent, everywhere, especially any in London. Imagine ringing Kenny Dalglish and saying Hi, I'm from Cameroon, can I come and take your picture please and could you wear a kilt so our readers back home will know you're Scottish. Geoff's last instruction from Harvey, the picture editor, had been to look out for something exotic, like an ostrich on a football pitch. That became the refrain of the week, every time we got really low.

I eventually got through to my so-called contact at Fecafoot. He was totally evasive. What did I want? What was the point of it? Who had given me permission? It was as if I was on a political investigation, trying to prove the President was mad, all Ministers were on the take, the country was in a state of collapse, instead of rejoicing in a happy event. You'd have thought they would be thrilled to have their achievements celebrated.

No, we couldn't see the team. No, dressing-room interviews were out. He was now going into a meeting. Could I see him after the meeting? 'I know when it begins, but I do not know where it will end.' Before he hung up, I got in one last request. I asked if we could at least have tickets for the press box. What? You know, so we can see the match? 'You can buy tickets at the gate.' Then he hung up.

In desperation, I did what any decent living British chap would have done. I rang the British Embassy. I asked for the First Secretary, ready to say any First Secretary, should I be asked. I talked hurriedly when a young-sounding and reasonably well-bred English accent answered. I rattled away, probably totally confusing him. It did sound a bit strange as I explained it, 10,000 miles for a friendly football match. He paused. Then he said he recognized my name. Didn't I used to write for *Punch?* Years ago, I said, but I was in. He would see us in an hour at the Embassy and try to help. Great, Britain.

It was hardly more than a suburban house, tin roof, white-painted, with a guard on the gate, but my heart leapt to see under a palm tree a Landrover with a Union Jack on the side.

He was called Brian Donaldson, Deputy Head of Mission, as well as First Secretary, originally from South Shields, but hard to tell as he's been serving the Queen round the globe for many years, watching shoot-ups from our Embassy in Bolivia to enjoying himself in Mauritius, his favourite posting so far. In just one hour since we had spoken, he had already composed and had typed out several letters to VIP people, summarising what I'd blurted on the phone, begging help for us. They were then despatched to various Government offices.

Then Brian got on the phone, chasing the recipients of his *billets doux*, and managed to talk a big cheese at the Ministry of Information into seeing us. We raced round, hung around, waited on various people's various pleasures, and by the end of the day we had a bit of paper in very pompous French allowing us to take photographs.

That was paragraph one. The next paragraphs listed all the things we could NOT photograph – this included the Presidential Palace, military places, telecommunication buildings, industrial zones, ports, airports and any place of strategic importance. Most worrying of all was a ban on anything they might construe as 'contrary to public morality or offend the dignity and honour of Cameroon'.

Bang goes your ostrich, Geoff. 'Actually, they don't have any,' said Brian.

We got a taxi first thing to the offices of Fecafoot, realising the only way to see people was to see people. In other words, turn up and wait. Phoning or writing was a joke. Just as it had been in London. This time we did have our bit of paper from the Ministry of Information.

Our impressive-looking Ministry of Information permit impressed the road police, but when we reached Fecafoot's offices, we were told sternly by another three-piece serge suit that it wouldn't get us far in football. I was continually amazed, in such an impossible climate, to come across this constant support for Savile Row. Football, he explained, comes under the Minister of Youth and Sport, not Information. Where was our pass from that Ministry?

More problems, more arguments. After a lot of waiting and persuading, it was agreed that an official would see us next morning.

The nation's superstar footballers were still proving elusive, hidden away somewhere from us, but the street level variety were everywhere. There were makeshift games on almost every space, between buildings, over drains, against the Cathedral walls, in amongst the stalls.

In taxis, we were always viewed with suspicion at first, but once I started my torrent of O-level French, explaining we were here to look at their football, it was smiles and laughs all round, slaps on the back and handshakes. They have little knowledge of our British teams and players, no more than we know about theirs. The only European names they know well are French, thanks to their cultural connections. To a man, their knowledge of England consisted of one word – hooligan. This always had them roaring with laughter.

While waiting to track down the footballers, I decided to track down the nation's leading TV sports commentator – Ben Berka Njovens. From Ben, I learned a great deal about football. Starting with English and Scottish football. His knowledge was incredible. As a boy, he had gone each week to the British Council Library and read all the sports pages. I was there, in the flesh, when England won the World Cup in 1966, and if pressed, I can remember the score. Ben knew the goal scorers, on both sides, the movements which lead to each goal, and the times when they scored. I tried him on Carlisle United, and he knew all about their season in the First Division. I asked him to name the ground where Hearts play, which he got, and the manager of Rangers. 'Glasgow or Berwick?' he said.

He was short, rather plump, rather vain, very self-confident, but very likeable. He went to Yaoundé University, did a broadcasting course, then joined the TV company five years ago, just when it was starting. Today, it is still limited to Wednesday to Sunday evenings only, from six to midnight, but their studios are very modern and well-equipped. They broadcast in both English and French. Ben is the main English language sports commentator.

Cameroon Radio and Television will be sending just seven people to Italy for the World Cup. There will be two TV and two radio commentators (to cover French and English) plus three crew. I imagine about 1,000 TV and radio hacks will be going from Britain, probably about 10,000 from Brazil.

Like everyone in Cameroon, Ben is very proud of the country's last and only appearance in the World Cup. This was in 1982. They were unbeaten, drawing with Peru, Poland and Italy, the eventual winners. That makes them unique. They are still the only country in the world not to lose a match in the World Cup finals. At some stage, every other country has been beaten, in at least one of the finals.

'I think the 1982 team was more gifted. We had a few stars then, such as Roger Milla. But our present team can turn it on when they want to. We have the robustness of England and Germany, the tactical acumen of Italy, the skill and fantasy of the South Americans. When we play well, we can steamroller the opposition and prove very hard to beat. Best of all, when the chips are down, we deliver. We can play badly, and win. There's often no justice in football. Just like life.

'But tell me about Hoddle. What did Bobby Robson really have against him? It always struck me that Hoddle did not deserve to be English . . .'

I arrived at Fecafoot at the arranged time, feeling hot and shivery, convinced I was going down with flu, if not typhoid or malaria. Geoff was feeling better now. He had decided his tummy trouble was caused by some ice cubes in a Coke. He should never have had them without checking they had used bottle water. Some patent pills brought from London were keeping the worst of the runs at bay.

MINISTERE DE L'INFORMATION
ET DE LA CULTURE

DIRECTION DE LA COMMUNICATION

SOUS/DIRECTION DE LA PRESSE

N° 323/MINFOC/DC/SDP/SRC.-

Réf. :

REPUBLIQUE DU CAMEROUN
Paix - Travail - Patrie

YAOUNDE, le 06 FEV. 1990

LE MINISTRE DE L'INFORMATION ET
DE LA CULTURE

A

Monsieur EDWARD HUNTER DAVIES
s/c Ambassade Grande-Bretagne
YAOUNDE

OBJET :Autorisation de photographier.

Monsieur,

En réponse à votre lettre par laquelle vous avez sollicité
une autorisation de photographier :

PHOTOS TOURISTIQUES

J'ai l'honneur de vous informer qu'aux termes du décret
présidentiel n°74/179 du 9 Mars 1974, les prises de vues photographiques sont libres sur l'étendue du territoire de la République
du Cameroun.

En conséquence, aucune autorisation préalable de photographier ne pourra être exigée.

Toutefois, certains points du territoire tels que les
Palais Présidentiels, les installations militaires et télécommunica-
tions, les zones industrielles, les ports, les aéroports et tout autre
point sensible ou stratégique ne pourront être photographiés que sur
notre autorisation spéciale.

En plus, les prises de vues contraires aux bonnes moeurs et
à la moralité publique susceptibles de porter atteinte à la dignité et
à l'honorabilité du Cameroun sont formellement interdites.

Enfin, vous veillerez à ce que l'ordre public ne doit point
troublé par vos activités photographiques.

Veuillez agréer, Monsieur, l'expression de mes sentiments
distingués./-

Le Ministre de l'Information
et de la Culture
P. Délégation
Le Directeur de la Communication

Eugène NDJIKI-NYA
Journaliste Principal

Photographic authorisation from the Cameroon Government: give or take a few restrictions

I have come to see your President, I said. Too late, an official replied. He has left for Douala. Along with the team, for tomorrow's match.

We were still with no tickets and no passes. Worst of all, we had now discovered we were IN THE WRONG TOWN. Sorry about that, Geoff. I suppose it must have been my fault. On the phone from London, I was sure I'd been told the friendly match against the Russians was in Yaoundé. I had not realised that two matches against the Russians had been arranged. The first took place in the National Stadium in Yaoundé the day before we arrived. The next was tomorrow, in Douala, some 200 miles away.

We considered hiring a car and driving on the main road, till we were told it was the most dangerous stretch of highway in all Africa, if not the world. There are wrecks all the way, littering the edges of the jungle. After dark, lorries drive with no headlights down the middle of the road. There are buses, but they too are driven by maniacs. We failed to find the train times, so that left the plane. We spent hours ringing and pleading, and at last got two seats for the first plane next morning, at eight o'clock.

In Douala, we went straight to Novotel Hotel where we were told the President of Fecafoot was staying. He had just popped out, so a girl on reception told us. Not again.

Geoff wandered around, looked over the swimming pool, checked the gardens, lining up likely places where he might photograph the team relaxing after training. I sat guarding the cameras, trying to look occupied. The hotel was full of working girls, slinking around, desperate for my custom and my room number.

After an hour, I asked another reception clerk if they knew where the Football President had gone. 'To the Falaise Hotel, probably, to see the team.' Oh no. Not another mistake. We jumped in a cab and went straight round.

The Falaise was a less imposing hotel, with a small reception area and a modest bar. Slumped on all the available chairs were the players, exhausted after training, sitting in their track suits, trainers, T-shirts. I recognised the look, that angle of their bodies, the boredom in their faces, just like footballers anywhere in the world, ones I have met from London to Milan. They were about to go into a team talk with their coach. Hence the heavy boredom. A blackboard with a pitch chalked on it was being carried through.

I didn't dare talk to them without first seeing the President, or I might ruin everything. It could even be a hanging offence. So we stood around, waiting. One or two players did smile and look interested, realising we were foreign. I was carrying two video tapes of English football highlights, bought in Woolworths.

At last the President came downstairs, dressed in a three-piece dark suit, with another official, the one I'd already spoken to. I rushed over and blurted out my name and business. They walked on, into the bar. I followed, trying to explain our purpose once again..

We all sat down and I was asked for any paper and permissions. I handed over everything I could find, down to my Camden Borough Council Discount Swimming Pass, my Spurs Member's Card and a BBC pass, three years out of date, from the day when I presented a book programme on the radio. Each item was very seriously studied. I also had a letter from the editor of *You*, in English and French, to Whom it May Concern, plus our pass from

the Minister of Information. I even let him see copies of the letters from the British Embassy which had been sent in our name, but never replied to. He took these last letters with him and put them in his pocket.

'And what is it you want?'

'To photograph the team,' I said.

No reply, no reaction, so I took this to be permission.

'And to have a press pass for the match.'

The assistant paused, watched the President for clues, then said this would be arranged locally.

'And can I have a few words with you, Sir,' I added, 'if I may, your excellency.'

I thought this would flatter him, and would help our cause.

'What about?'

'Oh, just a few questions.'

'Such as?' asked his assistant. 'We must have all questions listed first.'

'Oh, I dunno,' I said, never having thought of any questions. 'Well, how long have you been President, how you feel about getting into the World Cup finals, what the team's preparations are from now until then. That sort of thing.'

The assistant recited them all, one by one, making notes in his mind. I waited. Silence.

'You see, all very harmless questions,' I smiled, getting out my notebook. I looked up expectantly. More silence.

'The President can't answer them now. You will have to wait till much later. Come to his hotel at nine o'clock. When the match is over.'

The team were very friendly. They had seen me talking to the President and therefore assumed everything was in order. There were 22 of them, the home-based members of the national squad. Another ten or so were still abroad, playing in Europe, but would be joining later, in time for their African tour, and then Italy.

Cameroon's two best known, two most successful players at present are both goalkeepers. What a problem for the coach. And what arguments this causes on terraces throughout the Cameroon. Everyone has their own opinion about who should be Number One. Joseph Bell is the better known as he plays for Bordeaux, currently top of the French First Division. Playing in France means good coverage back home. Thomas Nkomo plays in Spain, for Espanol, not such a successful team, currently in their second division. The links with Spain are not so strong, so his games are not as well reported.

Bell is an extrovert, loud and showy, who jumps about his goals. Like Bruce Grobbelar, he can be brilliant one moment, then make a silly mistake. He can also be easily lobbed by rushing out too quickly. Nkomo is considered a quiet gentleman, calm and sedate, who might not pull off such dazzling saves, but is very hard to beat.

In defence, they have Emmanuel Kunde, the only player remaining from the 1982 World Cup squad. He is know known as the Old Lion. The national team is called *Les Lions Indomitables*. In newspaper headlines, or TV bulletins, they are always referred to as the Lions. A little boy in the street, wearing a national shirt, will be a *Petit Lion*.

The other star players are Ebwelle, an attacking defender; Ebongue, who is very fast; and Omam Biyik, their main striker. The captain is Stephen Tataw.

The home-based players are all classified as amateurs. Their clubs find them a job and accommodation, but don't pay any wages. They do however get a fairly decent win bonus, in Cameroon terms, so if you are with a successful club, such as Canon or Tonnerre from Yaoundé, or Union of Douala, then you might be able to double your salary. The jobs the clubs provide are fairly modest, such as mechanic or clerk, which pay around £100 a week. The top players might earn around £200 a week, counting their win bonuses – not a lot compared with our £2,000-a-week star players in England, or £5000 a week in Italy.

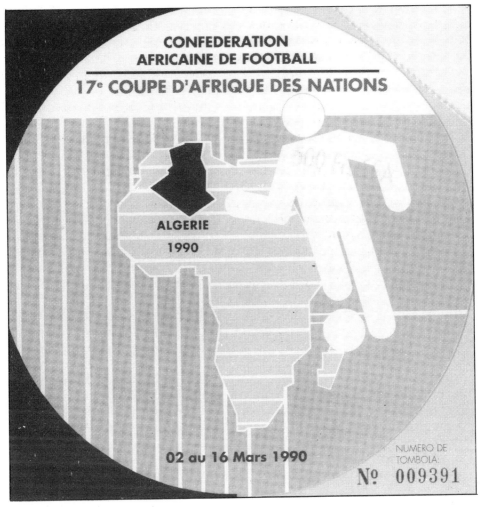

Stephen Tataw, the captain, plays for Tonnerre and works during the day as clerk at the TV station. He is an Anglophone – an English-speaking Cameroonian – one of the very few in the squad. He is tall, solid, with a little moustache. A couple of seasons ago, so he said, someone from Queen's Park Rangers was after him, but nothing came of it.

I then talked to two younger players, Alex Djomo and Victor Ndip. After the photograph round the pool, they walked off hand in hand, as many players did. Perfectly naturally. They even agreed to hold hands for another shot. Imagine British footballers doing that.

Victor works in an office each day from seven o'clock in the morning till midday. He then goes training with his team, Canon. Then back to work from two-thirty to six o'clock. He gets 150,000 local francs a month, or around £90 a week. His win bonus is 50,000 francs. If they lose, he gets nothing. He hasn't got a car. 'Only four players in the whole squad have got a car.'

The coach of the national team is Russian, Valerie Neponiachiv. The previous coach was French. He was on a huge salary, said to be almost £100,000 a year. He lived for three years in an expensive hotel, as no house in Cameroon was found to suit him. Valerie, the present coach, comes free – paid for by the Russians, as a goodwill gesture. He was the one who got them into the World Cup.

The deputy coach is an ex Cameroon star player, Jean Manga Onguene, holder of over 100 caps and the Balon D'Or award for the best player in all Africa. He was very helpful, despite being ill that day, with a stomach bug. He apologised for giving us so little time. He now had to take the tactics talk, and then it would be lunch and rest, before the match.

At the door of the team's hotel, a few boys were hanging around. Not for autographs, but to sell newspapers and tombola tickets. Inside, at the bar, were a couple of sports reporters, sitting waiting.

And that was where we stumbled upon the Yves, the Incredible Hulk. From the moment we met, he practically took us over. 'I am the Sports Voice of Africa! I am Free! I tell the truth! I am afraid of no one!'

He was small and fat, backslapping, teeth flashing, with a word and joke for everyone. And everyone did seem to know him,or at least his voice. Kom Yves Leopold is the main sports commentator for Africa No 1, headquarters in Gabon, a French language commercial radio station which is heard all over Africa. He promised to make sure in the hours before the match that we saw everything we might want to see, from football to eating and drinking. After football, those were obviously his two main hobbies. As the day progressed, and we went from bar to bar, where he always ordered the largest drinks, more of his friends joined him, who also ate and drank heartily.

We took Yves to photograph him at a local football pitch, the Akwa Stadium, used for Second Division matches. It is an old stadium, with the stand and most of the seats semi-derelict, but a groundsman was busy on the pitch, getting it ready for the next match. He was in bare feet and stripped to the waist, working his way slowly round the edges with a rake and barrow, smoothing out the pitch. The surface was all sand, with not a blade of grass anywhere. A tropical downpour earlier that morning had turned most of it into a mudbath. Most pitches in Cameroon are like this. Only two in the whole country have grass.

In the old stand about 30 men and young boys were lying down, stretched out on the benches, resting in the shade. In one corner of the ground, amidst a pile of rubbish, an old man was asleep, with giant, red-headed lizards crawling around him.

There was a simple scoreboard, which consisted of a bit of wood with the word 'BUTS' written on top, meaning Goals. The ground had a proper gated entrance and a concrete wall all the way round. I studied it carefully, looking for graffiti. I had been told there was never any trouble or hooliganism, but I was sure some lads must have let rip with a few scrawled words. I could find only one example. "AH, ÇA VA MIEUX. MERCI ASPRO'. It was daubed in white paint, the same sort of sprayed-on lettering you see in British grounds. I asked Yves if there was a hidden meaning I was missing. He looked as puzzled as I was. Did it refer to a jingle on local television? No, they don't have TV commercials. It could only have been simple irony. Watching their local team would give anyone a headache. How sweet. Much nicer than the racist or obscene words you see everywhere on the walls round White Hart Lane.

YAMBEN SIMON DIDIER

We went into the little dressing-rooms underneath the stand, and into the offices where there was an official from Fecafoot, absorbed in his paper work, like a good bureaucrat. On a wall into the dressing-room I noticed a printed poster, aimed at all players. 'LE FAIR PLAY C'EST LE RESPECT DE

L'ADVERSAIRE'. The notice had been put up by the association of 'un sport sans violence and pour le fair play'. I was amused, and at the same time a bit depressed, to see the use of the English words 'fair play'. It is a concept now totally removed from British football. The professional foul now ruins the British game. Our so-called undeveloped brothers are the ones trying to promote English virtues.

We got to the main stadium for the Big Match at six o'clock, an hour before kick-off. A bar owner we had met called Epanlo Dieudonne, drove us there in his large black Mercedes. He parked it just outside the main gate, only the second car to be parked there. Several thousand eyes were watching us. All around were poorly dressed, undernourished boys, sitting on a dusty embankment. He left the Mercedes, giving it not a second thought. I told him in Britain you wouldn't dare do that. It would either be stolen or vandalised, just for the fun of it.

There were amateur matches taking place all round the stadium, on any bits of open ground, some organised with posts and referees, watched by several thousand people, others were just kick arounds. Some were all-women games. There were people selling bananas, pineapples, sweets and strange-looking cakes, carrying their wares on their heads. In every direction, I could see people playing or watching football, all enjoying themselves. I felt a passing pleasure at being British, givers of the game to the world. I only wish it gave all of us such harmless pleasure today.

We went inside the stadium, down gloomy concrete corridors, peeped into the primitive changing-rooms, then positioned ourselves just inside the main gate to see the teams arrive. The Lions arrived first, crammed into a minibus. A supporter managed to get in behind the bus, before the gates were closed, and was manhandled by police and soldiers wielding nasty looking flexible truncheons. Above our heads, there were hundreds of spectators in the open-topped stadium. Some of them whistled and jeered. Then when the team emerged they shouted STE-PHEN, STE-PHEN, wanting the captain to give them a wave, and then VAL-ER-EE, the coach. Both obliged with a smile.

I sat at the back of the VIP part of the grandstand, along with my Mercedes friend, leaving Geoff to capture the lads on the terraces and the coaches in the dugout. The heat was still overpowering, under the burning concrete, but almost all the VIP guests were in dark three-piece suits.

Their version of Wembley's Royal Box was a flat bit of concrete on which a row of old-fashioned dining chairs had been lined up. They looked identical to the ones my mother had during the war, with moquette seats and very straight long backs, the sort which everyone threw out the moment the war was over and decent furniture came in.

A metal fence separated our part from the ordinary grandstand seats, but various scruffy boys were managing to squeeze through, carrying makeshift trays and plastic carrier bags, hoping to sell drinks and cigarettes. I bought a beer, as I was desperate, but most people shushed them away, as if their presence might ruin the tone of the VIP area.

NGATO OLIVIER

When the Football President arrived, followed by the leaders of the local police and military, staggering under their ribbons and honours, we all stood up behind him, bowed, and said 'Monsieur, le President', waiting for him to sit down first. They sat on the dining chairs, in the front row, looking terribly important. The President was soon joined on his left-hand side by a young white man in slacks and open neck nylon shirt, a striking clash with all the black dignitaries. A spy from Bobby Robson's camp? Maradona's personal emissary?

The stadium was fairly empty when the match began, with people still coming home from work, but it was soon about a third full, possibly with around 20,000. It was only a friendly, after all, the second one in a week against the same Russian first division team, Koupagne. The Lions had won the first one by a penalty, 1–0.

During the entire match, there was no communal singing or chanting on

TSOBGNY KOPA PAUL ROGER
Président

the British pattern, no shouting of names, no abuse hurled at the teams. It reminded me very much of the crowd in a game I once watched in Moscow. Most of the time, they were silent. If the play was slow or boring, and there were too many back passes, then sporadic whistling broke out. What they seemed to enjoy best was their own players making a mistake, falling over, giving a bad pass, missing a good chance, and then they would scream with laughter, clutching their sides. I suppose this sort of ridicule must have just as bad an effect on the poor players as any ritualised invective. Even in the posh seats, people smiled at bad play and muttered 'Ce n'est pas possible.'

Cameroon won, one-nil, from a free kick which ended in an excellent header by Ebwelle. This did result in a good cheer all round. As a match, I didn't learn much. Neither side was taking it very seriously. Cameroon passed neatly, struck quickly when they got a chance, but their defence was weak. Stephen Tataw looked dreadfully slow and got himself into trouble by

trying to be flash in his own area. The second half was ruined as a spectacle by endless substitutions by both sides. The Russians were on their out-of-season winter break. The Lions were missing five or six of their best players, the European-based professionals who will make the final team for Italy.

At half-time, six heavily armed police in riot gear and heavy helmets scurried on to the middle of the pitch. They were all quite small and weedy and finding it hard to run, weighed down by their combat tackle. I thought at first they were heading for the terraces, as a frightener, but all they did was sedately escort the referee and linesmen to their dressing-room.

As we left the grandstand, I talked to the white man in short sleeves. He was a Russian, a diplomat from their Embassy. When he heard I was staying in Yaoundé at the Hilton, he said we must meet for a drink.

We went straight back to town afterwards, to the Novotel Hotel, for our appointment with M. le Football President. As arranged by him for nine o'clock. We sat around the bar for almost two hours, waiting. I rang his room, number 559, just in case I had missed him. From time to time, various girls came over to us, offering personal suggestions about how we might put in our time.

All week we had struggled with officials. It was going to end in the same way. Yet the team had won, playing very respectable football. There had not been a foul or nasty tackle in the whole game. Our one and only reason for coming to Cameroon was to rejoice with them.

Football generally in Cameroon is something the whole country should be proud of. Considering their primitive facilities, their unpaid, undertrained players, their lack of proper pitches, their appalling bureaucratic system, their success has been remarkable. They will give Argentina a good game, if not a fright. They deserve to win the World Cup itself, if just for achievement in adversity and their insistence on fair play. If they do get through the first stage, by some miracle, each player will get £10,000. That would hardly buy Maradona a new earring.

Cameroon football might be top-heavy and lumped with bureaucrats, but at least it is not spoiled by sponsorship or corrupted by commercialisation.

KAMGANG BASILE

Players don't have agents. TV does not dictate kick-off times. Manufacturers do not control club finances.

At eleven o'clock, I decided to pack up. I had lost interest by this time in exactly how long M. President had been at Fecafoot, or the other dopey questions I had given.

'When the next girl asks for our room number,' I told Geoff, 'Let's say 559.'

'We'll book all of them,' said Geoff. 'On the hour, all night long, that'll learn him.'

Back in my hotel bedroom, I managed to catch the closing news headlines on television. It said that tonight, at the Douala stadium, Cameroon and the Russians had drawn, 0–0. What? I was there. I saw the goal. At last. The heat must have got to me.

Next day, on the way to the airport, I got talking to the taxi driver. I said I'd been at the match and he nodded, nil–nil, he'd heard the score. No, I said. Cameroon won. A great header from Ebwelle.

He looked at me, thought hard, furrowed his brows, then he started laughing. 'That might have been the Real Score, 1–0. But 0–0 was the Diplomatic Score. Our Government does not want to offend our Russian friends. . . .'

Good joke. Or was it?

At the airport, the whole Russian squad was there, some 22 of them, getting ready to board their Euroflot plane, waiting on the runway. As they came through customs, they were almost totally obscured by packages. In one hand, each was carrying a large JVC video. In the other, they had a stereo. I said quick, Geoff, take a snap. In an airport? You must be joking.

So we didn't capture it, but it was my final mental picture. Citizens of a Super Power on a visit to a deprived, Third World Country. I bet they were surprised to find themselves coming away with goodies they can't buy at home. But Cameroon is a surprising place. Perhaps they will spring their biggest surprise in Italy, on 8 June.

1990

Football in the Nineties

YES THERE will be football in Britain in the Nineties, do not despair, do not adjust your brain cells, do not leave the stadium without first looking at our very wonderful football merchandising, in all colours, all sizes, to fit all pockets, as long as they are enormous.

THE CLUBS: There will be only ten full-time professional clubs left in the United Kingdom by 1999, two from London, two from Manchester, two from Liverpool, two from Glasgow, and two from somewhere really boring in the Midlands. Clubs will not travel, as travel is far too exhausting and is a waste of good sponsorship time. Nobody wants to go somewhere really boring in the Midlands.

DIRECTORS: Will each have a cream-coloured Roller, three in-car telephones, one GCSE pass, an ability to understand a *Sun* headline at six paces and be able to recite, while drunk, 'we have the best interest of the club at heart'.

CHAIRMEN: Will all have tear jerking photographs of themselves standing on the terraces in torn breeks with coal in the bath, proof that they have always supported the lads in blue/red/white/grey. (Fill in title of club as necessary.)

GAMES: Only derby games will ever be played, as market research shows these are the best attended. It also eliminates all travel. So Arsenal will play Spurs every Saturday in the season, Celtic will always play Rangers, etc.

Matches will last 18 hours, with intervals every 15 minutes to allow those in the executive boxes to watch the horse racing, sleep, count their dosh, refill, talk to their Bimbos.

Each match will therefore be spread across six days. Research has shown that it just makes no financial sense, Brian, to have multi-million pound assets which are paraded in public only once a week, innit.

MANAGERS: Will be 50 times more famous than any player, have their own palace, newspaper empire, TV series, gold mine, jewellery shop and will always be in conference.

PLAYERS: Each team will still play with eleven of those, but each player will also have his own team of eleven consisting of agent, lawyer, accountant, personal masseuse, hair stylist, someone to work the video, travel agent, clothes co-ordinator, PRO, marketing manager and someone to

open the lager. These advisers will be kept constantly warming up during each game, ready to come on and give expert advice when needed. No more than 300 advisers are allowed on the pitch at any one time.

THE KIT: Each team's strip will change design every 15 minutes, to tie in with the commercial breaks. Players will also be allowed to model the new strips for a maximum of five minutes in every 15 minutes of play. Obscene gestures, spitting, swearing, laughing by the opposition during these opportunities for posing will be heavily penalised.

Each player must always carry a personal telephone, Filofax, PCW, spare contract and spare opener. Each club will have an orthodentist on hand to attend to injuries sustained during opening which might adversely affect photo opportunities and/or kissing each other.

PROGRAMMES: There will be no programmes, as we used to know them. They will have become mail order catalogues. Team changes will be kept secret, in order not to upset Stock Exchange quotation and the Dow-Jones Index.

SPECTATORS: Only allowed in if they pay £30,000 per year for an executive box. Property developers will be given priority, or multinational corporations with loadsa friends and an entertainment account swilling with shareholders' money based in Monaco. Standard executive boxes will have TV, video, cocktail bar, conservatory, jacuzzi, swirl pool, dining-room and hot and cold running maids. Extras for those visiting from the Costa del Sol will include bullet-proof glass, armed guards and changes of passport.

HOOLIGANS: Each club, by law, will have to have ten ordinary human beings, classed from henceforth as hooligans, who will be kept in an open cage, well out of the way, given undrinkable tea, unspeakable latrines, herded by rottweilers and beaten every time they use any disgusting language, such as 'But we're True Supporters' or 'Why did you sell Hoddle?' These hooligans will provide sound effects and 'atmosphere' for the executive boxes' stereo system and will be held responsible for our lads getting stuffed in the 1994 World Cup, plus everything else wrong with football, as we used to know it, Brian.